JOURNEYS
FELICITY NUNLEY
WITH
ROBIN GUNN & LORI PRESSMAN

This book was written, edited, and prepared for publication at the Arbor Center for Teaching at Arbor School in Tualatin, Oregon. Mary Elliott and Sarah Pope designed this book.

Copyright © 2016 by the Arbor Center for Teaching

All rights reserved. No part of this book may be reproduced in any form without permission in writing from the publisher, except by a teacher for fair use in the classroom or by a reviewer who may quote brief passages in a review.

Nunley, Felicity, Robin Gunn, and Lori Pressman.

Journeys (Arbor Thematic Curriculum).

Summary: Curriculum introducing studies of human journeys—historical, mythological, and imaginary—and animal migrations, with emphasis on mapping and dramatic play, to kindergartners and first graders at the Arbor School of Arts & Sciences.

ISBN 978-0-9821363-9-3

Printed in the United States of America by Lightning Source, Inc.

1 2 3 4 5 6 7 8 9

INTRODUCTION

It turns out that the most important work in developing a curriculum is deciding what *not* to teach. At Arbor School we have not been afraid to assert that some ideas are more worthy of consideration than others. When imagining what is attractive to young children by way of curricular content, it is easy to fall victim to simplistic thinking. Since the children are small and immature, the concepts and content they are thought to be able to manage can end up being narrow and unsophisticated. Subjects so local and limited as to defy a bright-eyed child's deep curiosity litter elementary curriculum binders. One of our central beliefs, however, is that students care about and therefore deserve to learn about big ideas, seminal ideas. From the start it has been our intent to devise a meaningful curricular framework that asks students to engage deeply with the concepts that form the backbone of the disciplines. These concepts, in increasingly refined and elaborated iterations, spiral up through the class levels. While review of that framework is constant, the long threads that we first identified as essential continue to form the tapestry of the children's studies. Critical ideas, concepts, and works from history, science, and literature constitute the thematic core and are played out over the nine years a student spends at Arbor.

We thought long and hard in the construction of the school's thematic curriculum about just which conceptual threads ought to be picked up for the elementary school-age child. In devising each step of the curriculum, multiple considerations came into play. Are the ideas generative for the age child we wish to engage? Are the topics ones these students can come to care about? Are they dynamic enough to allow for in-depth study with ample room for individuals to make choices of importance to them? Are they rich and stimulating, with opportunities to create connections across domains and disciplines? What fundamental concepts are at work that can be built upon as the child matures? Are those concepts central and lasting? How can the ideas be used as vehicles for inquiry and expression, as topics for reading and writing, as sources for mathematical exploration, as material for rendering with line and color, for fabricating in three dimensions, for transformation through music?

To meet the surprisingly wide-ranging palates and marvelously global wonderments of children, we created a program that focuses on big ideas, on topics that can be linked under the umbrella of still larger central themes in human understanding—on seasons and cycles, energy and motion, communities, inventions and discoveries, pattern and diversity, cultures of the world. We ask students to think about the sun and shadows, the reasons for the seasons, the adaptive advantages of camouflage and mimicry, the role of plants on the face of the Earth, the sea change that Galileo and company engendered in our understanding of our place in the cosmos, the phases of the Moon, the cascade of events that followed the Louisiana Purchase, the flow of energy in nature, the connections between physical geography and culture, the conditions that preceded the emergence of the notion of natural law, genetics and evolution, the forces that bind humankind into societies, Newtonian mechanics, the physics of static structures, the structures and systems of animal organisms, a selection of the defining stories—from the *Epic of Gilgamesh* to the *Mahabharata*, from the *Odyssey* to Anansi tales—of the world's peoples, the rise of the monotheistic religions, geologic time, and what we understand of the workings of our own minds.

The knowledge and creativity of faculty members bring these larger themes to life. Drawing together their deep understanding of the developmental realities of each age group and a well of background knowledge that grows with each encounter with the subject matter, Arbor teachers plan irresistible experiences for their students, building strong structures of skill and knowledge and understanding. A thorough treatment of the philosophy, principles, aims, and teaching practices that support this curriculum is available in our book *The Idea of Arbor School*.

Many of our thematic units have been illuminated in rich detail by Arbor teachers' articles in Cambium, our journal of curriculum and pedagogy; relevant articles are included in this volume, but every issue is also available for download at arborcenterforteaching.org. The Primary Journeys year is perhaps best understood in the context of our whole K-8 Theme cycle, a sketch of which follows.
 –*Kit Abel Hawkins, Arbor School Founding Head*

The Arbor School Theme Cycle
 PRIMARIES (K-1)
 Year 1: Seasons & Cycles
 Plant Cycles: Seeds, Roots, & Shoots; Flowers & Fruits; Decomposition; Seasonal Change
 Critter Cycles: Animals Preparing for Winter; Frogs & Butterflies
 Human Cycles: Houses Around the World; Human Body Systems; Winter Solstice

 Year 2: Journeys
 Sink & Float: Boats; Imaginary Journeys; The Mayflower
 Migrating Animals: Whales
 Greek Mythology: The Journey of Odysseus; The Golden Apple
 History of Arbor School

 JUNIORS (2-3)
 Year 1: Change & Continuity
 Geologic History, the Rock Cycle, Earth Science
 Electricity & Magnetism
 Weather: Clouds, the Water Cycle, Wind, Temperature, Storms
 Time: Clocks & Calendars

 Year 2: Communities
 North American Physical Geography & Paleontology
 First Americans, First Oregonians, Human Migrations
 Colonization, Lewis & Clark, the Oregon Trail
 Early Settlement of Portland
 Portland Bridges

INTERMEDIATES (4-5)
Year 1: Environments
Ecological Niche: the Arbor Campus
Habitats & Adaptations: Oregon
Ecosystems, Biomes, Climatic Regions
The Human Body
Oceanography

Year 2: Inventions & Discoveries
The Ancient Western World (Sumer, Egypt, Greece, Rome)
    Early Developments in Writing, Counting Systems, Building Principles, Astronomy
    Mythology, Epic Poetry
    Ancient Architecture
The Middle Ages in Europe
    The Rise of Islam
    The Three Estates of Medieval Society
    Arthurian Legends & Historical Fiction
    Tessellations & Stained Glass
    Simple Machines & Fundamental Mechanical Principles
The Renaissance in Europe
    Brahe, Copernicus, Galileo
    The Mathematics of Science
    The Printing Press
    Portraiture
    Optics
    Mapping

SENIORS (6-8)
Humanities: Peoples of the World
Our three-year program in Humanities seeks to help students discover the myriad ways in which all people are similar and to celebrate the ways in which we are different. We do this by examining each major area of the world through a wide selection of fiction and nonfiction readings (by native authors, if possible), through guest lectures and film presentations, through magazines and newspapers. We study and prepare traditional foods and enjoy music, dance, and the arts, going out into the community to public performances when possible. Each year we mount a significant production that integrates Humanities studies as well as requiring cooperative growth.

We follow six main threads as we study each area of the world, particularly considering the ways in which they all intertwine:

1. *Geography:* We learn how the region was formed and examine how people interact with their physical surroundings. We seek to develop an awareness of place and an understanding of how people, goods, and ideas move throughout the area.
2. *History:* We aim for a sense of empathy for the past and understanding of the reasons for continuity and change. We try to include a full range of social classes in our studies, not just the kings and generals.

3. *Religion:* We consider the role of religion of in all human societies and its influence on history and seek familiarity with the basic ideas and ethical traditions of the great religions, including animistic ones. We recognize that all societies have ideals and standards of behavior and that people's ideas affect their actions.
4. *Culture:* We work to understand the concept of culture and how it is transmitted, developing appreciation for the rich complexities and differences between cultures. We focus on the special role of the arts in reflecting the inner life of a people and how they project an image of a people to the world. We study myths of origin, legends, and stories of heroes and heroines.
5. *Society:* We try to understand family, community, and nation, discussing the structure of social classes and comparative political systems as well as the complex relationships between peoples of the world.
6. *Economy:* We develop an awareness of economic issues from basic needs and wants to capital and markets, distribution, and consumption. We want students to be able to recognize and analyze the economic systems and interdependence of humans all over the planet.

Year 1: South Asia, Sub-Saharan Africa, China
Year 2: The Americas
Year 3: Eurasia

Science Cycle

The goals of Science are to make concrete and relevant the beautiful abstractions of science, to provide exposure to a wide range of topics, and to develop each student's confidence in her abilities to solve problems and draw conclusions from observations. Senior Science is built around opportunities to construct knowledge through lab experiments, demonstrations, field work, and student-designed investigations; it is also integrated with the concurrent theme in Humanities. For instance, the China unit might include a study of seismographs, gunpowder, and the construction of the Great Wall.

Year 1: Pattern & Diversity
Rock Cycle, Paleontology & the Fossil Record, Plate Tectonics, Evolution, Genetics

Year 2: Energy & Motion
Newtonian Mechanics, Electricity, Light/Sound/Water Waves, Renewable Energy

Year 3: Systems & Structures
Invertebrate Biology, Atomic & Molecular Structures & Interactions, Human Nervous & Endocrine Systems, Statics & the Strength of Materials

PRIMARY AIMS

Cover page: Primaries muster their courage to cross a footbridge in the Arbor Woods. Photo by Lori Pressman.

PRIMARY AIMS

"A journey of a thousand miles begins with a single step." –Lao Tse

The five- and six-year-olds entering the Primary years at Arbor School are at the beginning of a long journey. Most of them are quite freshly launched into a life of reading and writing and using numbers. So we have a special job to do. We must make this start meaningful and captivating, real and purposeful. Regardless of curricular content, we must make it obvious that the hard work of learning to read and write and calculate is worth their while, and we must build the foundation for a life of thoughtful inquiry and expressive communication supported by the habits of an independent learner. By embedding our instruction into rich thematic content, we provide our students with an inviting arena in which to practice their fledgling skills.

We seek to use children's natural inclinations to kindle enthusiasm for the work of learning to form good questions, do research, collect data, and share new knowledge in clear and creative ways.

Make and do: Primary students are doers by nature. We strive to provide them with many authentic and active experiences: to compare the tuft of fragile, stringy roots on a cosmos plant with the thick, ropy taproot of the dandelion; to taste the toothy crunch of the *Mayflower's* staple hardtack. We touch and feel the baleen of a whale, finding precise language to describe its smooth and flexible surface and imagining how to replicate it in a model.

Relish stories: Primaries love stories. They love stories about people they know, but they also love stories set in faraway places or long, long ago. They love to be read to, and they love to imagine themselves into the stories they hear. During our study of the Greeks, our dress-up area is stocked with togas and lightning bolts, laurel crowns and grapes. When we study the journey of the *Mayflower*, the children take on the characters of William Brewster, John Howland, and Rose Standish, imaging their hopes and fears, misfortunes and triumphs. A deep dive into stories teaches empathy, and inhabiting a character makes it easy to soak up historical details.

Collect: Primaries need big pockets. Treasures are waiting at every turn: purple berries on autumn bushes, well-formed mud balls, a shiny candy wrapper, the perfect stick. Intriguing facts are equally ripe for the plucking. The size of the world's largest carrot, the length of the small intestine in adult humans, or the miles of an Arctic tern's astonishing migration— Primaries cherish these facts, turning them over in their minds like shiny stones. And once we've gathered in all that data, we can sort and classify it and make comparisons, whether we're grouping whales by their feeding style or making visual representations of the distances travelled by migrating animals.

Experiment and practice: Anyone who has lived with a six-year-old learning to whistle knows that children this age love to practice. They naturally experiment and when their tinkering leads to success, they try to replicate it, then replicate it again. They love the feeling of mastery and, as a basketful of perfectly folded paper airplanes can attest, they love mass production. We capitalize on this impulse, helping Primaries find similar satisfaction in well-crafted handwriting, observational drawing, or a math game that never seems to grow old— all the while nudging them to the next level of sophistication.

Think big: Primary-age children present us with seeming contradictions: they fizz with the excitement of a birthday party but thrive in the comfort of a "regular" day's routine. They are literal and myopic, but also ask big questions: "Where was I before I was born?" "How do you make water?" While certainty is satisfying, Primaries are able to chew on a surprising amount of ambiguity. It is important not to underestimate the scope of their intellectual appetite. We teach them to distinguish between "lightning" questions that can be quickly answered with a bit of research and "meaty" questions that will lead to a cascade of inquiry and related investigations.

INQUIRY AND EXPRESSION

A successful Theme offers multiple points of entry for inquiry and wide-ranging choices for constructing and demonstrating durable understanding:

Reading Aims
- Listen attentively to books read aloud, tracking a story over multiple reading sessions and/or extracting important information
- Identify beginning, middle, and end in stories
- Explore theme, genre, character, setting, and narrative arc
- Gain independence in exploring nonfiction titles
- Appreciate history as a story

Writing Aims
- Write to communicate
- Report with growing attention to specificity and detail
- Hone letter formation skills and practice conventions of print that support legibility
- Develop stamina for recording ideas, stories, and new knowledge
- Craft stories that follow a typical narrative trajectory
- Use guess-and-go spelling in the service of fluency while also learning and applying spelling conventions
- Label (diagrams, maps, etc.) to cement new vocabulary and to practice scaling print size to available space and considering the placement of text on the page

Researching Aims	Apply background knowledge to new topics of study
	Wonder
	Hone questions to generate fruitful lines of inquiry
	Record new knowledge
	Distinguish fiction from nonfiction
	Learn to navigate nonfiction resources
	Distinguish important facts from intriguing but non-essential information
	Gather facts and develop basic organizational strategies
	Synthesize information and show understanding by being able to restate facts
	Develop a sense of the scope of history and compare human experiences across time
Problem-Solving Aims	Make predictions based on background knowledge
	Provide evidence to support predictions and conclusions
	Use number lines, time lines, diagrams, charts, tallies, etc. to organize and understand information
	Use manipulatives and other tools to build numeracy skills and represent numbers in increasingly abstract ways
	Develop understanding of scale, relative size, and units of measure
	Extract numerical information from word problems
	Use drawings to plan, design, make sense of information, and show thinking toward a solution
	Apply new knowledge to iterative design
	Develop an array of strategies for solving a problem, whether in mathematics, design, or social interactions

JOURNEYS

HABITS AND ATTITUDES

A successful Theme also provides opportunities for students to develop ever more sophisticated habits and attitudes:

Expanding world view: Exploring the immediate environment is a full-time occupation for the youngest children. The Primary-age child is ready to expand her horizons to consider faraway places and unfamiliar customs. She is delighted to learn that the tooth fairy is a bunny in China or that traditional Japanese houses had walls of paper. She is interested to learn that Greece is a real, modern country and to try pronouncing the word for *watermelon* in Greek. Discovering that there are many ways of doing things can be a powerful lesson to the Primary child, who can sometimes be wedded to current understandings and resistant to change.

Wonder and appreciation for the natural world: Hearing stories of the critters who share our planet and observing them close at hand, children naturally become stewards of the world around them. In turning the chicken eggs in an incubator, keeping a careful record of the temperature and humidity inside the box, the children take a hand in maintaining a healthy environment for the developing chicks. They know that tiny lives hang on their actions and care. When we study whales, the Primaries are incensed to hear about plastics littering the oceans and often become ardent and vocal activists for protecting the health of the seas. At this age, stewardship begins to expand beyond children's immediate horizons.

Spirit of investigation: In studying subjects that are removed from their own lives by place and time, Primaries must develop means of exploration beyond direct experience to satisfy their curiosities. Students learn to turn to books for information as well as pleasure; we help them develop such early research skills as listening for important details, marking relevant pages, identifying key facts, and practicing basic organizational strategies.

Focus and attention: As engaging as we have sought to make our curriculum, as much as we wish to invite wonderful flights of fancy and creative approaches to projects, part of the work of school is learning to follow instructions, listening carefully and internalizing expectations so that one can act independently and judge the quality and completeness of one's own work. Students must build their stamina for effort within given parameters rather than working hard only in pursuit of their own ideas. Throughout the Primary years we look for strides taken in this realm, and we find that the thematic curriculum keeps the work welcome and pleasurable for most children.

Whether focused on the plants in our backyard or the food of countries half a world away, we hope that thematic studies awaken curiosity in our students and compel them to embrace the possibilities that the world presents.

BROAD PURPOSES OF THE JOURNEYS YEAR

Studying journeys provides rich opportunities to explore and extend what Primaries are naturally about. The Journeys theme leads us to learn about times and places other than here and now, to consider the experiences of others, to dissect the structure of narrative tales and craft our own, to use and make maps, to look for patterns and order in the world and develop a sense of wonder at nature's designs. We begin with child-size, hands-on whimsy: building a watercraft for a tiny felt mouse each student has received as a companion for summer adventures. The idea of a sea voyage leads us to a scientific investigation—what properties make an object sink or float?—and also plunges us into some great adventures, from the history of the *Mayflower* voyage to the legend of Odysseus's tortuous travels home from Troy. We think about the stages of a journey, from planning to packing to taking the trip to returning home, by conjuring and mapping our own imaginary islands and then writing a travelogue as we set out for a visit. We also study some incredible animal journeys, researching the migrations of caribou, salmon, Arctic terns, and gray whales.

Journeys naturally compel us to write about our experiences, and learning to write is one of the greatest aims for our Primaries. It takes hours and hours of practice to form letters, to order them into words and march those words along the page to tell a story or record an observation. The list of things we write under the banner of our Journeys theme is impressive and varied: postcards, packing lists, map keys, adventure stories, *Mayflower* journals, whale fact cards, books of Greek gods—among many others. This curriculum also offers encounters with many kinds of reading material. We read adventure stories beyond number, looking for the pattern of home-adventure-home and learning about narrative arc in the process. We read lots of nonfiction, both scientific and historical. In fact, the lines between fact and fiction are not at all clear to Primary-age children, and the Journeys content offers new wrinkles: How do we know what happened 400 years ago on the *Mayflower*? How do we even make sense of a number like 400 years? Is the *Odyssey* real or made-up? Or somewhere in between?

Numeracy practice unfurls in every unit, too. On the *Mayflower* there were 102 passengers, three masts, and two dogs; the journey lasted 66 days. Building a life-size replica of a blue whale and calculating the distance of an Arctic tern's migration reveals not only the astonishing power of those creatures but also the way numbers efficiently illustrate facts and events: The distance from my house to school is seven miles. A caribou migrates 700 miles. Numbers become a new means of expression for children to articulate their understanding of the world.

The centrality of story in this curricular year provides added impetus for this new class of children to begin to create the story of their school years together as a crew. Through living into the drama of John Howland's rescue on the *Mayflower* or of Hera's jealous antics up on Mount Olympus, the Primaries come into unforgettable new relationships with one another and their shared story begins to unfold. Years later, the whole group still remembers who played Zeus in the Greek play, who birthed baby Oceanus on board the *Mayflower*. These experiences color their shared history and cement their bonds as a class.

The trajectory of inquiry outlined on the following page doesn't conform precisely to the unit-by-unit descriptions in this book, but seeks to reveal the rich soil in which we invite Primaries to dig throughout the year.

1. How can we represent the three-dimensional world with a paper and pencil? What tools can we use to get somewhere we've never been before? What are landmarks? What do you recognize that tells you you're close to home or to school?

2. What makes an object float? What makes it sink? How do materials behave differently in water than they do when they're dry?

3. What is a journey? How do you prepare for one? What do you need to know about the place you're going? Why do people make journeys?

4. Who else makes journeys? Why do some animals migrate? Why don't all of them migrate? How far is 25,000 miles? How do we make sense of such an enormous number? How can a little bird possibly fly that far?

5. How can we classify whales by the way they eat? How are whales' lives like our own? How are they different? How big is a blue whale, really? What makes these giant animals so vulnerable and how can we help?

6. What is history? What was life like in the past? What objects did travelers on the *Mayflower* use that we don't use now, and what items do we take for granted that hadn't been invented yet in the 1600s? How long ago did the *Mayflower* journey happen in comparison to other events and eras? How would it feel to leave your home forever and seek a new home?

7. What is a myth? How is it different from other stories? How is it different from history? How can we tell the difference between history and myth? What was the world like in ancient Greece? What is it like in modern Greece? Why are we still so interested in the stories the ancient Greeks told? How were the gods and goddesses like humans?

A GUIDE TO USING THIS BOOK

The large units that shape our year are described in these pages with the intent to capture the most essential content, purposes, and lines of inquiry we pursue. The projects undertaken by students in any given Journeys year will vary according to the needs and interests of learners and teachers. In describing each unit, we have used the following categories to reveal what's most important and what might ensue.

Essential Questions

The essential questions are the motivating force behind the projects that we decide to complete in any given year. These are questions that we hope children are able to answer after the completion of the unit, whether or not they are aware of the questions' existence. We use the questions to help us create projects that have depth, contain multiple points of entry, and inspire students. They allow us to have consistent goals from year to year while maintaining the flexibility to tailor the projects to the needs of our particular cohort of students.

Unit Aims

The goal of all of our projects is to extend children in the realms of intellect, character, and creativity, to build skills and knowledge, compassion and cooperation, planfulness and care in execution. In this section we describe our more tangible expectations as well as the habits students will be practicing.

Deepening Knowledge and Honing Skills

This section gives an overview of many of the projects that have helped our classes meet our goals, but is given as inspiration rather than prescription. We expect the content of every unit to flex from year to year in the service of each new class's particular needs and interests and according to special opportunities their teachers may wish to incorporate.

Assessment and Evidence

At Arbor, assessments are not used to arbitrate success or failure, but to provide repeated practice and shine a light on skills that need tending. At the Primary level there is a particularly broad array of developmentally normal trajectories as children build their capacity and skills to reason and communicate. Gathering evidence of their individual progress is a reflexive, almost subconscious process in the life of the classroom, and that evidence is not always easy to quantify. The pride on a child's face the morning she becomes a "second-sider," writing so much in a journal entry that she has to flip over her paper to continue the tale, is as real a marker of achievement as the wobbly letters themselves. It speaks of a sense of authorship that is earned only by stamina, grit, and an exciting new capacity to broadcast ideas. "Formal" assessments—whether in the shape of weekly reading conferences or math story problems drawn from Theme studies—tell us a great deal about a student's thinking, but we are just as keen to notice children's interactions as the curriculum spills into their play and to hear them exclaim in happy recognition when a read-aloud fits the "home-adventure-home" arc we've been studying.

We practice backward design in devising our curriculum, asking ourselves what we're hoping to see in students' development—and how we'll know if we're seeing it. Since our habit is to begin with the desired outcome, in this guide we've opted to spotlight a few pieces of student work in each unit and reveal how we might assess them rather than creating more general matrices for student accomplishment. What does a child's account of life on the *Mayflower* tell us about his empathy? Can we find evidence that he's taken to heart our encouragement to add "juicy details?" If we see technical excellence but little imagination, how can we craft an invitation to more fully embrace his character? The examples we've included are not meant to be prescriptive, but we hope they show the depth of Arbor teachers' delving for better understanding of their students. Our aim is always to support student growth and development in a way that conveys to children that joy and effort matter—and to articulate appropriate "next steps."

Connected Content

Articles our teachers have written for Cambium, our journal of curriculum and pedagogy, serve to illustrate more minutely what might transpire during a particular unit. Pertinent Cambium articles therefore appear in full at the end of each unit in this volume. They have been adapted slightly to fit the layout of this guide, and each article originally appeared in a collection of related material from across the school, so you may wish to download a PDF of the whole issue from our website at www.arborcenterforteaching.org/publications.

Standards Alignment Analysis

Each unit in this volume has been analyzed for relevance to the skills, habits, and knowledge identified by the Common Core Standards, the Next Generation Science Standards, and the National Geography Standards as critical for development in kindergarten and first grade. The results of this analysis have been printed in an appendix at the end of this volume. The Standards served by the unit's material are listed in separate tables for Literacy, Math, Science, and Geography. We have not reprinted the Standards' descriptive language in full, but have quoted enough to aid educators needing a quick reference. In many cases the Standards shift only marginally from one grade to the next, so we have chosen to amalgamate them and paraphrase the descriptions. If assessment based on the Common Core Standards is central to your teaching practice, please be sure to refer to the Standards' full text.

Arbor Thematic Curriculum guides incorporate each discipline only as it intersects with Theme work; much of our teaching in every academic realm is therefore beyond the scope of this volume. If, for instance, the Math Standards alignment for a given unit seems slender, this indicates that the Primaries' math work is less closely tied to our theme in that portion of the year.

UNIT 1:
MOUSE BOATS AND BUOYANCY

Unit cover page: Mouse Watching Me at Swim Lessons, by Cole P.

MOUSE BOATS AND BUOYANCY

We all feel more comfortable entering a room with something in our hands. This is precisely the reason kindergarten and first-grade students are assigned the task of building a boat for a small stuffed mouse that they bring to school on the first day. They are given no guidance about design for the boats except that they should use materials that they can find around the house. On the first day, in come soda-can catamarans, bark rafts, sailboats, and rubber band-driven propeller crafts—some more seaworthy than others when we test them in the waterways of the sculptural fountain and the goldfish pond out front. The shared experience gives the children instant common ground; admiration of a classmate's clever interpretation of the assignment quickly leads to working together at Choice time or an invitation to play at recess.

And the mice? Early in the summer, each child has received a hand-stitched mouse in the mail from the Primary teachers, along with directions for writing a postcard about some adventure with the mouse. The postcards, with their charming illustrations of Mouse at Swim Lessons or Mouse Having Surgery After Being Chewed by the Dog, hang in the classroom when the children enter. These tales provide more fodder for conversation and connection with new friends, and the mice themselves sometimes become the focus of recess play.

Hand-sewn felt mice ready for summer adventures with the Primary class

JOURNEYS

ESSENTIAL QUESTIONS

- What does it look like when something floats? Sinks? Partially sinks?
- What materials sink and float?
- What properties help an object float?
- What features help a boat float?
- What household objects and tools make a good boat?
- How can you design and build a boat to hold objects that don't float?
- What are some ways to propel a boat?
- What are some different ways of solving a design challenge?
- How can you ask questions or give appreciative comments about a peer's work?
- How can you answer questions and receive compliments graciously?

UNIT AIMS

During Mouse Boats and Buoyancy studies, students will:

General Habits	Connect with classmates and see themselves as part of a community
	Learn to give and receive supportive comments
	Ask questions
	Practice being patient and flexible as they work with others
Reading & Writing Skills	Write a very brief adventure story
	Record sink/float experiments on paper
	Listen to read-alouds pertaining to the theme

Math & Science Skills	Experiment with objects that sink or float
	Make predictions based on background knowledge
	Use drawings to show the stages and results of experiments
	Provide evidence to support predictions and conclusions
	Count objects 1:1 and in groups of tens and ones
	Sort and classify objects according to one or more attributes
Design Skills	Express creativity and individual design sense in an open-ended project
	Investigate the properties of various materials
	Plan for use of a small space (a postcard) that must accommodate both writing and illustration
	Use real tools for boat construction
	Draw from observations
	Apply new knowledge in iterative design of boats for sink/float experiments
Other Skills	Practice presenting to the whole class

DEEPENING KNOWLEDGE AND HONING SKILLS

The beloved Arbor mouse tradition began many years ago with an artist parent named Maggie Rudy, who taught others to sew diminutive felt mice with pipe cleaner limbs so that each new Primary could be welcomed with a special friend. (Arbor eighth graders have been known to take the stage at graduation with that same little companion tucked in a pocket for old times' sake and for courage in delivering their speech.) Maggie later elaborated on the project herself and eventually began a photography blog and a career illustrating children's books with her minutely detailed mouse characters in clever dioramas.

The summer postcard assignment gives us a first look at new students' writing and drawing abilities. Finding the right words to tell about a mouse's adventure in the brevity demanded by the format, planning how to use the space to leave room for an address, even just separating the words and the picture onto different sides of the postcard—all this is new territory for rising kindergartners and still good practice for returning first graders. The mouse boats are a natural extension to launch students on a nautical year of curriculum; they also allow teachers to observe New Hands' natural design proclivities in an open-ended project.

In the classroom, we immediately set up a gallery of our mouse boats around the room, touring them to admire their wide array of imaginative and practical features. Each child is armed with a treasure hunt worksheet to find boats with a flag, a leaf, a crow's nest, a paddle wheel, a hammock, etc., carefully printing the builder's name in the appropriate square. Everyone practices giving and receiving supportive comments and asking and answering questions about the boats. Taking turns to introduce themselves and point out their boat's features, the children feel what it means to command the attention of the class—with warm and gentle support from the teachers for those who need it—and to listen attentively to their peers. The Primary classrooms then visit each other's boat museum, forging connections across the whole grade.

Thinking about boats naturally leads us to wonder about objects that sink and float. We test floating objects around the classroom, practicing making predictions and recording results and then revising our ideas—who would have imagined that the metal cap would float while the plastic boat sinks? Will a Lego piece float? What about natural materials gathered from the woods and orchards? We begin to consider the properties that let a boat sink or float, launching a design challenge to see how many pennies we can load on a tinfoil boat before it sinks. Children notice that a flat bottom adds stability and high sides are important to keep the water out, but a double layer of foil doesn't necessarily help. They sketch successful designs and are inspired by friends' results to improve their own prototypes. We watch as the experiments continue outside at recess, with new boats built in the Junk Box being tested in the ponds on in the watercourse of our Rill sculpture, and learn a lot about our new class's enthusiasm for tinkering. Mouse couture workshops often spring up during Choice time or Open Design periods, letting us glimpse certain children's deftness with needle and thread and others' pleasure in sketching elaborate outfits.

Partnership with Parents

Assigning a design challenge for summer homework tells us much about our young students' families. If a scale model of a tall ship complete with rigging or a boat with a working propeller sails in the door on the first day of school, it's likely that more experienced hands have shaped the design and construction. We are vague about how much help parents should give with this assignment because we hope to learn more about their natural style of guidance. Do they give the child complete freedom in the planning and execution of the project? Do they work alongside the child, offering support but not inserting their own ideas? Do they get swept up in the fun of crafting and tinkering to the degree that the child is doing little of the work himself? We don't praise or admonish any of these stances, but over time we hope to steer parents to a middle ground, assisting in the procurement of materials, helping the child think through his ideas, teaching enough about the proper use of tools to keep the child safe, but always encouraging independence and letting the child hone his own creative vision—sometimes by experiencing real frustration when best efforts fall short and having to muster the grit to try again or the flexibility to imagine a different but equally satisfying outcome. This relationship between parent and child will be critical in creating a successful environment for homework in later years, and annual independent projects are particularly fine opportunities to practice finding the right balance. We tell Arbor families that we envision elementary education as a three-legged stool, supported equally by the efforts of the student, the school, and the parents.

ASSESSMENT AND EVIDENCE

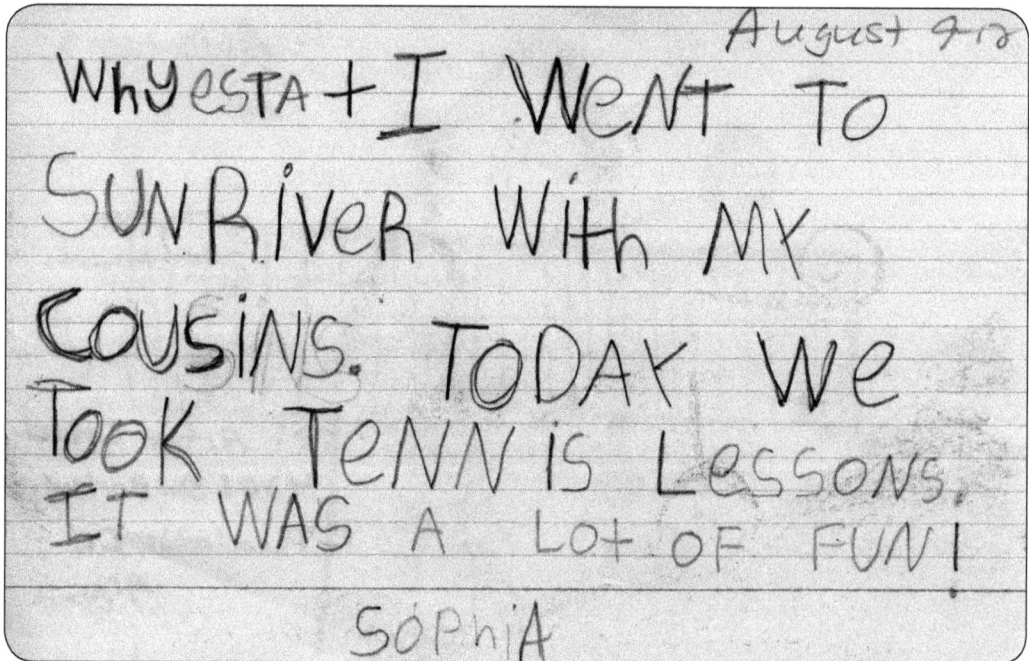

Sophia's postcard shows strong artistic ability, neat and legible letter formation and spacing, and careful placement of text on the page—leaving room for the address on the verso is a tricky spatial concept and also a physical challenge for children already laboring to confine their words to a smaller-than-usual canvas. Most mouse postcards we receive arrive like this one, with the address wedged in wherever a parent can manage to place it without obscuring the child's text or illustration.

This sailboat has a rubber band propulsion system and deck railing made by looping rubber bands around nails driven into the deck.

This bark boat has a tinfoil hot tub mounted on the foredeck and a hammock slung under the pavilion in the stern. The mouse can hang her laundry from the clothespins glued to the roof.

CONNECTED CONTENT

Cambium Vol. 2 No. 1: "Setting Sail for School: A Voyage of Discovery"

Relevant Cambium articles are appended at the end of each unit. To read this one in its original context, please download the full issue "Home to School, School to Home" at arborcenterforteaching.org/cambium.

BIBLIOGRAPHY

**Boat Books:
Nonfiction**

Borden, Louise. *Sea clocks, the story of longitude.* New York, NY: Simon & Schuster, 2004.

Kentley, Eric. *Boat.* New York, NY: Dorling Kindersley Publishing, 1992.

Lincoln, Margarette. *Amazing boats.* New York, NY: Knopf, 1992.

Phillips-Birt, Douglas. *The love of sailing.* London, England: Octopus, 1976.

Spectre, Peter H. *Wooden ship: the art, history and revival of wooden boat building.* Boston, MA: Houghton Mifflin, 1992.

Picture Books

Allen, Pamela. *Who sank the boat?* New York, NY: Coward-McCann, 1983.

Bang-Campbell, Monika, illus. by Molly Bang. *Little rat sets sail.* New York, NY: Harcourt, 2002.

Conrad, Pam, illus. by Richard Egielski. *The lost sailor.* New York, NY: HarperCollins, 1992.

Crews, Donald. *Sail away.* New York, NY: Greenwillow Books, 1995.

Domanska, Janina. *I saw a ship a-sailing.* New York, NY: Macmillan, 1972.

Lippman, Peter. *Busy boats.* New York, NY: Random House, 1977.

Stead, Philip Christian. *Jonathan and the big blue boat.* New York, NY: Roaring Brook Press, 2011.

Todd, Traci N. and Sara Gillingham. *T is for tugboat: navigating the seas from A to Z.* San Francisco, CA: Chronicle, 2008.

Tagore, Rabindranath. *Paper boats.* New York, NY: Macmillan, 1992.

Mouse Picture Books:

Aesop, *The town mouse and the country mouse.*
    Lorinda Bryan Cauley, Jan Brett, and Helen Ward have all retold and illustrated this classic fable. Comparing versions is an interesting lesson in itself.

Battut, Eric. *Little mouse's big secret.* New York, NY: Sterling Publishing Co, 2011.

Dijkstra, Lida, illus. by Piet Grobler. *Little mouse.* Asheville, NC: Front Street, 2003.

Henkes, Kevin. *Lilly's big day.* New York, NY: HarperCollins, 2006.

Henkes, Kevin. *Wemberly worried.* New York, NY: Greenwillow, 2000.

Kuhlmann, Torben, tr. by Suzanne Levesque. *Lindbergh: the tale of a flying mouse.* New York, NY: North-South Books, 2014.

Lionni, Leo. *Frederick.* New York, NY: Pantheon Books/Random House, 1967.

Lobel, Arthur. *Mouse soup.* New York, NY: Harper & Row, 1977.

Lobel, Arthur. *Mouse tales.* New York, NY: Harper & Row, 1972.

Numeroff, Laura Joffe. *If you give a mouse a cookie.* New York, NY: HarperCollins, 1985.

Pfister, Marcus. *Milo and the magical stones.* New York, NY: North-South Books, 1997.

Rudy, Maggie. *I wish I had a pet.* New York, NY: Beach Lane Books, 2014.

Rudy, Maggie. *The house that mouse built.* New York, NY: Downtown Bookworks, 2011.

Steig, William. *Amos & Boris.* New York, NY: Farrar, Straus and Giroux, 1971.
    A whale and a mouse save each other's lives and become the truest of friends. This touching book with its toothsome prose is an Arbor favorite.

Steig, William. *Doctor DeSoto.* New York, NY: Farrar, Straus and Giroux, 1982.

Walsh, Ellen Stoll. *Mouse paint.* Orlando, FL: Harcourt, Brace, Jovanovich, 1989.

Cambium

INNOVATIVE K-8 CURRICULUM FROM THE ARBOR SCHOOL OF ARTS & SCIENCES

SETTING SAIL FOR SCHOOL
PRIMARIES (AND MICE) ON A VOYAGE OF DISCOVERY

by Robin Gunn

We ask students to take risks each day that they enter our classrooms. The first day of school is no exception as children filter into the rooms that will house a bulk of their learning, wearing a patchwork of trust, vulnerability, and willingness on their sleeves. What if, as they enter, they do so with a physical object that creates a common ground, a connection to their new classmates? What if, when they glimpse the walls of their classroom, their drawings and handwritten names are already settled there? Objects and pencil markings made at home, couched in support and trust, now stand in our classrooms as symbols of welcome and of our promise to nurture the risk-taking that is learning.

These goals provide the framework for the summer homework at Arbor. For Primaries (kindergarten and first-grade children), who will soon embark on a year of "Journeys" curriculum, the invitation to set sail comes in the form of a mouse. This is a very particular mouse, constructed of felt and pipe cleaners under the dexterous fingers of parent and teacher volunteers and sent via post. The arrival is prefaced with a letter detailing two assignments: for the children to design and create a water vessel for their mouse, one that they can carry in their own hands, as well as to send two postcards to their teachers telling of their summer adventures with their mice. After all, a trip to the grocery store or tagging along for a swim lesson can be quite an adventure for such a little mouse.

As the year progresses, Primaries will journey to imaginary lands, take on the identities of passengers on the Mayflower, study the migrations of animals, and follow the voyage of Odysseus.

"Mouse mail" is a welcome sight as the postcards fill our mailboxes in the latter part of summer. Children tell their stories in ways that are comfortable for them. Paris drew a picture of Jordan, her mouse, tucked in a colorful purse for security on the roller

JOURNEYS

coaster. Griffin covered the front of his postcard with a picture of a kickball game that depicts the players and his mouse, Red. Many a mouse visited grandparents in such states as Ohio, Montana, and California. Whether near or far, these journeys were recorded, celebrated, and finally displayed around the room in anticipation of the first days of school.

As for the second assignment, to create a mouse-size water vessel, we must wait until the calendar page flips to September. When the time comes these brave Primaries arrive with their boats carefully cradled in arms or held in the protective cup of two hands. The adventurous mice make their debut within frameworks of cleverly constructed materials. Nina's clay boat, shaped by her hands, has two toothpick benches and an anchor that can be tossed off the bow. She reports that the benches double as seat belts. Jack points to the bundle of branches that form the hull of his raft, made seaworthy by an impressive amount of hot glue. Peter used both glue and tape to transform coffee cans, cardboard and yogurt cups into a comfortable vessel. He lifts up his boat to reveal twelve carefully placed corks he feels will ensure his boat's flotation. Maddie excitedly demonstrates how her sail moves from one side to another, the mast solidly glued to a painted pie plate.

And so the day begins. The goals of this summer assignment are specific, but the process lends itself nicely to the interests and learning styles of individual children. We are asking students to find their own way into an assignment and then to share the finished product with us. They are learning an invaluable skill: to take a task designed by someone else and make it their own.

Henry's classmates and teacher admire the rubber band propeller on his bottle boat.

A bridge between home and school is created, too. The process the children completed at home and the journeys they took during the ten weeks of summer all hold a story, a sense of knowledge gained, a burgeoning expertise about the ways of felt mice and of boat construction. Each individual joins the larger group with valuable contributions gleaned from experience. Those first conversations, whether between student and teacher, among peers, or from family to family, are often initiated across the bridge of the "mouse experience." First-day anxieties ease as children admire features on classmates' boats or commiserate about the challenges of gluing together seventy-eight popsicle sticks. New friends find commonalities in the anchors they have made out of clay or steering wheels of cardboard. They gather around a large tub of fabric, shoulder to shoulder, fashioning outfits for their mice. Whether a mouse dons a pipe cleaner scarf to keep warm or a purple cape to fly speedily through the air, whether a boat has a tinfoil flag or a mesh hammock, these Primaries enter with something held in common. That shared experience forms an important first step in what will become our collective journey as a Primary class.

Nili demonstrates her mouse boat's features to Sophia and Maddie

The mice and boats provide inspiration for activities that foster a sense of community within the newly formed group, as well as opening our yearlong theme of Journeys. The Primaries pair up to draw each other's boats. They report back to the group on details, such as fishing nets and propellers, that their classmates just shouldn't miss. There are lively discussions about what makes a boat float as children rally for corks, wood, paddles, and engines. "Sink and Float" experiments fill the room with excitement and surprise at the floating block and the sinking eraser. The children do an inventory of their boat materials to find that seventy-eight popsicle sticks were used on one, while twenty pompoms were used on another. Boat scavenger hunts, a boat museum in which each Primary class presents their work to the other, and games that sort and classify boats fill our day as we make the most out of having these water vessels as centerpieces in the classroom. And inevitably, someone wonders aloud whether his boat will safely carry his mouse down the rapids of the Rill, a sculptural stone watercourse built just outside the door of our classroom. A new adventure is hatched—perhaps the mice should now send postcards detailing the thrills of life at school!

Want to make felt mice for your own classroom? Instructions are available for download here: arborcenterfor teaching.org/s/ FeltMice.pdf

We hear from families that stories of these activities are told in after-school car rides, at the dinner table, or in those sleepy moments just before bedtime. The bridge, it would seem, is open in both directions as the Primaries find ways to bring their school experiences home.

UNIT 2:
MAPMAKING

Unit cover page: A map of home by Solomon O.

MAPMAKING

Maps will be a constant in a child's years at Arbor, whether he is scaling up a Mercator projection of the whole earth and discussing the strengths and weaknesses of that representation or plotting the course of Saum Creek through our woods. At the Primary level, maps are essential for a good journey. We begin with a very familiar trip: from home to school. Thinking about roads and landmarks—the homes of carpool mates, a doughnut shop, a hospital, a field full of alpacas, a bridge—each student maps his daily commute. Making a map requires patience, a keen eye, and sophisticated spatial awareness. Each map tells us something about the mental territory of the mapmaker, too. The individual mapmaker's perceptions shine clearly in each map: one child might include the community garden in her neighborhood; another is careful to include her best friend's house. Perhaps evidence of parental habits, one student's map included no fewer than three coffee shops!

Mapmaking isn't a self-contained unit within the Journeys curriculum; it forms part of the work for every other focus of our studies in this year, whether we are tracing an Arctic tern's sinuous circuit of the globe or Odysseus's adventures amongst the islands in Greece. Making and reading maps requires discrete skills that we teach directly, however, so for the purposes of this guide we have chosen to consolidate our aims for Mapping studies here.

ESSENTIAL QUESTIONS

- What clues help us recognize where we are?
- Why do humans make maps?
- What can a map show us?
- How do you read a map?
- What are the key features of a map?
- How does a compass work?

UNIT AIMS

During Mapmaking studies, students will:

General Habits
- Develop spatial sense and powers of observation
- Build accuracy in recording observations

Research Skills
- Identify the essential features of a useful map
- Use maps to locate specific places
- Use maps to trace animal migrations, beginning to relate climate information to different areas of the globe

Reading & Writing Skills
- Interpret a diverse array of map types
- Build sight-word recognition of geographic terms
- Practice labeling features of hand-drawn maps, scaling print size to available space and considering the placement of text on the page

Math & Science Skills
- Learn basic geographical terms and compass directions
- Practice using a map key and coordinate system for reading maps
- Learn about magnetic north and practice using a compass
- Navigate a simple coordinate grid
- Encounter and experiment with concepts of scale and ratio

Design Skills	Draw simple maps, considering distances and relative positions of landmarks
	Model 3-D landforms in clay
	Draw compass roses
Other Skills	Appreciate maps as powerful tools for communication
	Develop the habit of recognizing and using maps in everyday life

Primaries working on home-to-school maps

JOURNEYS

DEEPENING KNOWLEDGE AND HONING SKILLS

To a young Primary student, the idea that she is *somewhere* is not immediately obvious. Her feet are on the ground, or in a tree, and where that ground or tree is exactly in relation to other places is not necessarily very important until the desire to be somewhere else arises. The habit of standing outside oneself enough to imagine a "bird's eye" perspective is novel and tricky and trumped by the immediacy of being in the tree. When we ask them to draw a map of their journey to school, it quickly becomes obvious that Primaries come in two models: those who have never noticed anything out the window of their car and those who have noticed every detail at every intersection.

For the Primary child, mapmaking is inextricably related to storytelling and action. As the child draws his route to school, he animates the map with the sound of the car engine, adding bumps in the road with a swoop of his line. Important landmarks like the school's mailbox or the neighborhood baseball field are writ large, leaving visual evidence of the child's interests and priorities.

We look for maps in books, noticing how it colors our understanding of life in the Hundred Acre Wood to see the relative positions of Pooh's house and Piglet's house, with the Heffalump trap in between and Eeyore's gloomy place off in a swampy corner. We teachers draw large maps to amplify the studies at hand and set the students to work in shifts, coloring or illustrating and gradually developing a sense of the myriad Greek islands or the lonely span of the North Atlantic between England and Cape Cod.

Studying maps gives us the chance to introduce the vocabulary of geography. Children are already familiar with the mountains, hills, and rivers that surround and bisect their city; now they learn about bays, peninsulas, archipelagos, capes and deltas. Collections of maps provide opportunities for reading and for comparing maps that have different purposes—a map of Disneyland, a map of China, a conceptual map of a child's day. We learn to examine the map key or legend and practice making symbols to represent important landmarks on the maps we draw.

In some years, we make three-dimensional maps in clay and overlay them with the simplest of string grids—A, B, C and 1, 2, 3 are coordinates even the newest readers can work with, and tangible topographical features are easier to comprehend than place names or symbols on a paper map. *Which square is the mountain in? Which three squares does the river cross?*

We draw compass roses, chanting "Never Eat Soggy Waffles" and watching the needle spin toward magnetic north on a real compass. In the Junior years Arbor students will try their hands at navigation, and by the Intermediate years they will be surveying the campus; for now we aim only to introduce the concept of the cardinal directions. For young children who are still trying to grasp basic spatial ideas, untangling the notion of reliable fixed points versus self-referential directions like right and left is enough.

ASSESSMENT AND EVIDENCE

Joseph's map reveals his interest in the route to school—intersections, freeways, the hospital, coffee shops, and a playground are carefully and sensibly placed. This first grader is a fluent writer and made good use of space in labeling his landmarks where there was plenty of room for legible text. We note his addition of a compass rose, a map feature we studied in class concurrently, but didn't specifically ask the children to include on their home-to-school maps.

Juliet's charming map is dominated by outsized flowers and trees—more likely evidence of this kindergartner's desire to decorate the page than a representation of actual landmarks.

JOURNEYS

BIBLIOGRAPHY

Cyrus, Kurt. *The voyage of Turtle Rex*. New York, NY: Houghton Mifflin, 2011.

Fanelli, Sara. *My map book*. New York, NY: Harper Collins, 1995.

Gannett, Ruth Stiles and Ruth Chrisman Gannett. *My father's dragon*. New York, NY: Random House Books for Young Readers, 1948.

Hale, Kathleen. *Orlando the marmalade cat: a camping holiday*. New York, NY: Penguin, 1938/1990.

Hartmand, Gail. *As the crow flies: a first book of maps*. New York, NY: Aladdin, 1993.

Milne, A. A. *Winnie-the-Pooh*. New York, NY: Dutton, 1926.

Sís, Peter. *Madlenka*. New York, NY: Farrar, Straus and Giroux. 2000.

Sís, Peter. *Tibet through the red box*. New York, NY: Farrar, Straus, and Giroux, 1998.

Sobel, David. *Mapmaking with children: sense of place education for the elementary years*. Portsmouth, NH: Heinemann, 1998.

UNIT 3:
IMAGINARY JOURNEYS

Unit cover page: Imaginary islands by Charlie S.

IMAGINARY JOURNEYS

Nothing could be more natural to a Primary-age child than to imagine a voyage of adventure. Whether they are building forts, playing with stuffed animals, or creating a miniature world, children invent cultures, lands, and stories. The Imaginary Journeys unit capitalizes on that impulse and introduces some structures that we will use and refer to often in our Theme work all year. Most notably, we articulate the stages of a journey:

1) Have an idea
2) Make a plan
3) Make a packing list and gather supplies
4) Depart
5) Have adventures and misadventures
6) Return home

These basic stages of a journey will appear again and again in our studies throughout the year. This unit is packed with opportunities to practice literacy and mathematics and to begin trying our hands at recording our fictional stories.

ESSENTIAL QUESTIONS

- What is a journey?

- What are some different types of journeys?

- What are some reasons to go on a journey?

- What are the stages of a journey?

- What are strategies for thinking up an imaginary journey?

- What are the story elements in an imaginary journey?

UNIT AIMS

During Imaginary Journeys studies, students will:

General Habits

Practice being flexible in working toward common goals

Engage in creative thinking and be inspired by others' ideas

Apply acquired knowledge in ways that express individuality

Research Skills

Study a variety of maps, both fictional and real

Acquire and apply new vocabulary from studies of geography and navigation

Reading & Writing Skills

Listen attentively to chapter books read aloud, tracking a story over multiple reading sessions

Independently read or look at a selection of journey-themed books

Identify beginning, middle, and end in stories

Note Home-Adventure-Home story arcs

Record original story ideas in small, manageable chunks (daily logs, postcards)

Build writing stamina and practice guess-and-go spelling for longer words (packing lists)

Math & Science Skills

Learn basic geography terms and concepts, including cardinal directions

Identify and create map keys and coordinate systems for reading maps

Work with number combinations to 10 (shopping for supplies on a $10 budget at the Adventure Store)

Explore, identify, and create patterns, including ABAB, ABAC, and growing patterns

Solve math problems that involve patterns

Use math drawings, tallies, and manipulatives to solve problems

Design Skills

Practice flexible thinking and imagination in drawing and populating maps

Create models at different scales

JOURNEYS

DEEPENING KNOWLEDGE AND HONING SKILLS

We begin our imaginary journeys with mapping. What begins as an abstract drawing—a doodle of a prescribed number of small dots, large dots, straight lines, and curved lines—suddenly looks a lot like the maps we have been studying. The addition of blue watercolor gives us a never-before-visited archipelago of our very own. We add landmarks—mountain ranges, swamps, blueberry fields, caves—and the children begin to narrate stories about those places: only on the mountaintop are the natives safe from the whirlpool; this is where the Cyclops lives; beware of the poisonous sea otters that live on this peninsula. We make lists of safe and dangerous places, beautiful and hard-to-get-to places, all of which requires quite a lot of effort from small hands still getting accustomed to forming letters.

Reading *My Father's Dragon* heavily informs our work in this unit. We make a big map of Elmer Elevator's travels and the kids take turns to color it. We study Elmer's packing list, noting the contents of his backpack on chart paper and then checking off each item as he uses it. Then we make packing lists to visit our own islands. Some items are strictly practical, but you never know what might come in handy:

FRENDS
AVAPTRCAT (adventure cat)
ASODANdSheLD (a sword and shield)
Shus WITh SAKShinCAPS (shoes with suction cups)
FOWDANd WATR (food and water)

We lay in supplies—lava suits, grappling hooks—on a budget at the Adventure Store. Students gain practice at combining numbers that sum to ten. Most are already familiar with all the number pairs that make ten, but now they must consider sets of three or four or five or even more addends. Motivated mathematicians can take this exercise as far as they wish, finding more and more combinations—even if it might not be great travel planning to spend *all* one's money on five pairs of $2 gumboots, we applaud the thoroughness that drives a child to consider every possibility! Those who cannot yet make numeric calculations use math pictures to show their thinking.

Recording our island adventures requires journaling. How do we plan to travel—kayaking? Riding an eagle? Flying in a helicopter? Where will we land? What would we like to see? Once we arrive, adventures ensue. There are rivers to cross, witches to evade, giant owls circling overhead, prickly bushes to circumnavigate. Keeping a journal is perfect writing practice; each entry is a manageably finite exercise that can gain in length as stamina and skill increase. We return home with many tales to tell and children can't wait to read their adventures to their friends.

Chronology: Beginning, Middle, and End

Listen to any Primary-age child tell a story and you will find yourself following intently, trying to connect the dots of chronology. They weave in and out of events based on their own method of sequencing, often beginning with what was most important to their own experience. There is no place for linear retelling when your mom's friend let your family inside the elephant habitat at the zoo and you got to feed this monstrous creature from your own hand!

Guiding their minds through the sequenced process of a journey supports the Primaries in seeing the basic narrative arc of any story, in stepping beyond the simple lists of events or salient memories that tend to characterize their Weekend News reports. We think aloud about the steps to a journey and write our ideas up on big paper. They guide our imaginary journeys to islands with names like Flower and Shoe Island. First we saved money, then we planned our trip, then we made our packing lists, what is next? We read books with the theme of home-adventure-home and we write about this cycle from our own imaginary lands. When we are ready to set sail on the Mayflower, we compare the steps of our imaginary journeys to those of the passengers on this historic ship and someone exclaims, "It's a home-adventure-NEW home!"

Adding up purchases at the Adventure Store: a pair of gumboots plus two oranges

ASSESSMENT AND EVIDENCE

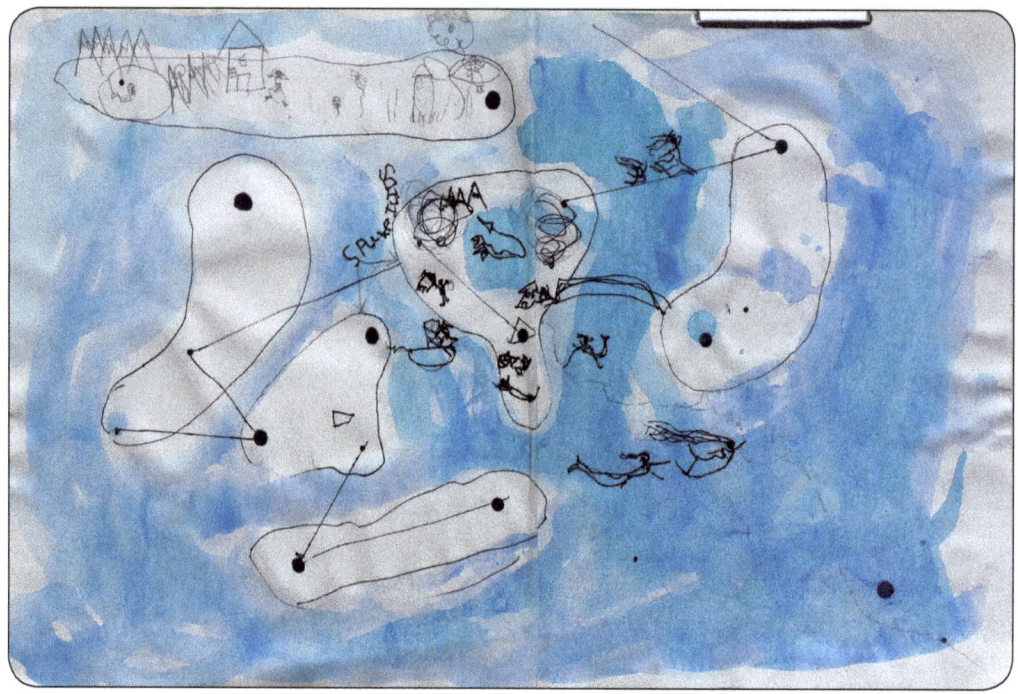

Noemi's map of Beautiful Island and Dangerous Island

For our kindergartners, this is the first invitation to make up a story and write it down—an opportunity for total creative freedom. Our first graders have new powers of stamina to record more elaborate tales. The results are wonderfully wacky. We watch what happens while they're working and talking, collaborating, making sound effects to go with their exploding volcanoes. Who can dig in and follow an adventure on the island? Here is Noemi's story:

IT WAS MONiNg Me ANd MY MAMA Were PLAiNg IN MY grDIN WeN SADINLe A GrAT CAT FLO DOWN ANd AskT Me To CAM I SeD yes IT hAD MY STAF I JAPT ON Then The GrAT CAT FLO SAW FAST ThIT We Were There IN LeS TheN one MINiT I JAPT OFF JAST TheN A GrL RAN BI She WAS yeLiNg BeKAS A hoWs WAS chASiNg hr I so A SkeLATIN WITh A BAG OF GLD I GOT The GLD I JAPT ON We FLO AWAY IN LeS TheN ONe MINIT I WAS home The END

"It was morning. Me and my mama were playing in my garden when suddenly a great cat flew down and asked me to come. I said yes. It had my stuff. I jumped on. Then the great cat flew so fast that we were there in less than one minute. I jumped off. Just then a girl ran by. She was yelling because a house was chasing her. I saw a skeleton with a bag of gold. I got the gold. I jumped on. We flew away. In less than one minute I was home. The end."

Noemi's tale of adventure clearly shows the home-adventure-home arc we've talked so much about. In keeping with the breakneck pacing, her illustrations show figures making balletic leaps across the page. The great winged cat, with drooping whiskers and curlicue tail, swoops in and out of the action.

CONNECTED CONTENT

Cambium Preview: "Home, Adventure, Home: Charting an Imaginary Journey"

This article is appended on the following page. To read it in its original context, download the issue "Mapping" at arborcenterforteaching.org/cambium.

BIBLIOGRAPHY

Home-Adventure-Home fiction:

Armstrong, Jennifer. *Lili the brave*. New York, NY: Random House Books for Young Readers, 1997.

Eastman, P. D. *Are you my mother?* New York, NY: Random House Books for Young Readers, 1960.

Gannett, Ruth Stiles and Ruth Chrisman Gannett. *My father's dragon*. New York, NY: Random House Books for Young Readers, 1948.

Heidbreder, Robert, illus. Kady MacDonald Denton. *A sea-wishing day*. Toronto, Canada: Kids Can Press, 2007.

Hobbie, Holly. *Toot & puddle* series. New York, NY: Little, Brown Young Readers.

Lobel, Arnold. *Mouse soup*. New York, NY: Harper Collins, 1977.

Martin, Jacqueline Briggs. *On sand island*. New York, NY: Houghton Mifflin, 2003.

Milne, A. A. *Winnie-the-Pooh*. New York, NY: Dutton, 1926.

Sendak, Maurice. *Where the wild things are*. New York, NY: HarperCollins, 1963.

Sís, Peter. *A small tall tale from the far far north*. New York, NY: Farrar, Straus, and Giroux, 2001.

Sís, Peter. Madlenka. New York, NY: Farrar, Straus, and Giroux, 2000.

Sís, Peter. The three golden keys. New York, NY: Farrar, Straus, and Giroux, 2001.

Sís, Peter. Tibet through the red box. New York, NY: Farrar, Straus, and Giroux, 1998.

Williams, Vera B. Three days on a river in a red canoe. New York, NY: Greenwillow Books, 1981.

Cambium

INNOVATIVE K-8 CURRICULUM FROM THE ARBOR SCHOOL OF ARTS & SCIENCES

HOME, ADVENTURE, HOME
PRIMARIES MAP AN IMAGINARY JOURNEY

by Felicity Nunley, Lori Pressman, and the Primary team

The Primary students at Arbor—kindergartners and first graders—distinguish themselves in many ways: by their small size, by their wonderment and passion as they embrace the school culture, by the trays of lovably misshapen oatcakes and cookies they proudly proffer all over campus on baking days, and perhaps most of all by the engines of their imagination. They transform the school into a fantasyscape. We nurture those powerful imaginations by bringing them to bear on the curriculum: in the years when Journeys are the theme of study for the Primaries, the students take on the personae of the historical passengers on the *Mayflower* and imagine themselves into every stage of the voyage.

In preparation for this undertaking, the Primaries begin in the fall with a study of maps. In September and October, writer-in-residence Melissa Madenski guided the students through a series of lessons inspired by David Sobel's *Mapmaking with Children* in which they made maps of their homes and of journeys from home to school or to another favorite place. These charts of the children's known world, their safe places, prepare them to map and explore the realm of make-believe with an imaginary journey to an unknown land. Their teachers lay the foundations during the summer by documenting a journey of their own. In 2007, lead teacher Felicity Nunley and reading specialist Robin Gunn received a grant to travel north for a three-day kayak adventure in the San Juan Islands. They photographed each phase of the trip, from the planning and packing to their return home, for a slide show and kept detailed journals of their experiences to share with the students. The class studied the arc of adventure stories in their teachers' trip and in literature, then applied that structure to their own imaginary voyages. In addition to mapping practice, this lesson string builds young students' skills in reading comprehension, writing, reasoning, using coordinates, and decomposing the number 10. It is a chance to stretch their imaginations, work independently, and share their creations and stories with the class. Bon voyage!

A teacher's journey can take place on a far more modest scale. Young children can appreciate the adventure in any outing; a drive to visit relatives or a weekend of camping can be ample fodder for discussing the stages of a journey. Be sure your trip involves a map or two, however simple.

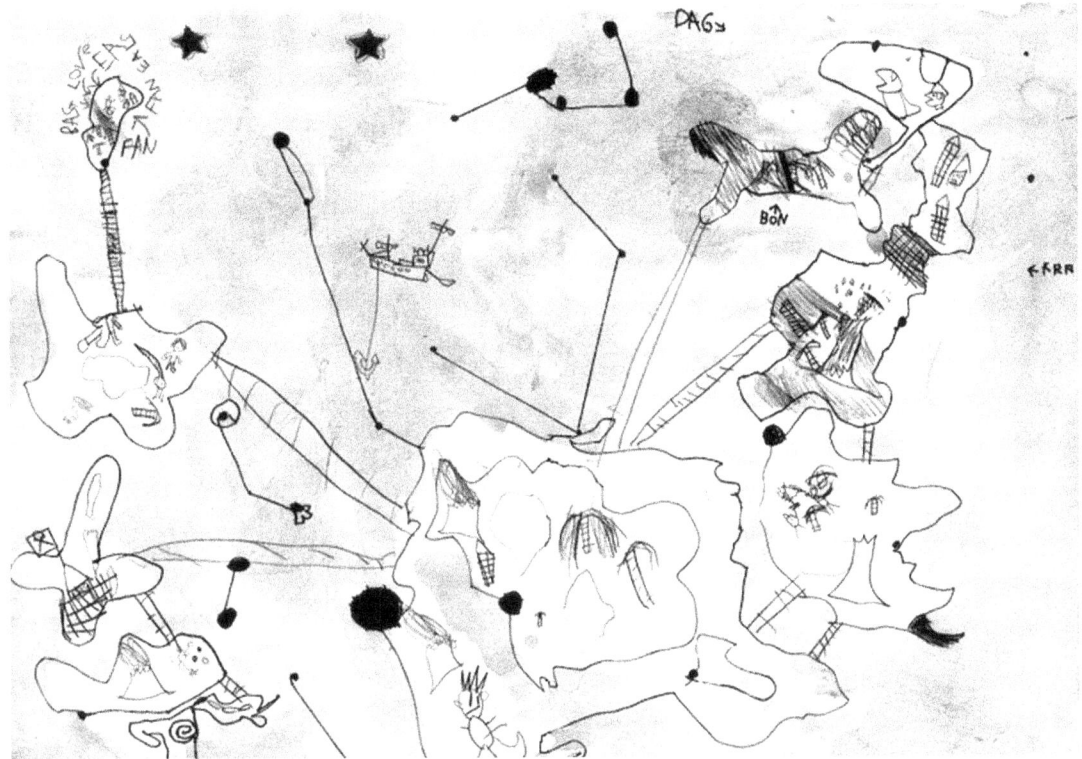

FORECAST

Day 1:
Read aloud *Three Days on a River in a Red Canoe*, by Vera Williams, to introduce the Home —Adventure—Home idea. Use the story to tease out the steps of a journey:
1. idea for trip
2. packing/planning
3. farewell
4. adventure
5. return home

This is a long story, and children will be eager to share commentary and their own boat ride tales.

Day 2:
Teacher's travels. Review the Home—Adventure—Home structure from Day 1. Show pictures of your journey, looking for evidence of the five steps and paying particular attention to maps of the trip. Ask children to bring in maps from home for Day 3, and collect a wide variety of maps and nautical charts to use as models.

Days 3-4:
Map drawing and painting. Distribute watercolor paper and permanent markers. Without explaining that they are making maps, instruct children to draw 20 small dots, 15 larger dots, 10 straight lines connecting some of the dots, and curved lines to surround groups of dots. Then encourage students to make a connection between their own drawings and the charts on the

Maps to collect:
Road maps
Symbolic maps
Nautical charts
Trail maps
Tourist maps
Topographic maps

Behind the Scenes:
Hang maps, particularly nautical charts, conspicuously near the working area.

Materials:
- Heavy watercolor paper for each student
- Permanent markers
- Blue watercolor paint
- Paint brushes

JOURNEYS 51

Field Notes:
Beginning the maps without understanding what they were drawing was a challenge for some of our literal thinkers; we wanted to loosen them up with a free, abstract exercise. We have found that if they know they're making maps, kids tend to jump prematurely to detailed images. As an experiment, we encouraged this slower unfolding and were pleased with the results.

walls: they have just charted a previously unknown group of islands. The children can decide which parts of their drawing will be land masses and which will be water. Paint water with a watercolor wash. As they spend time with their maps, they will naturally begin to invent the landscape and inhabitants.

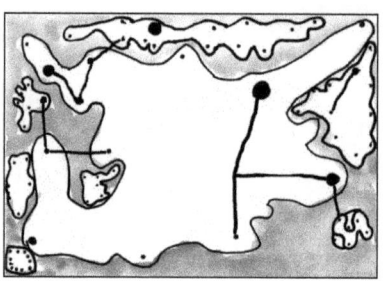

Day 5:

Read aloud *On Sand Island*, by Jacqueline Briggs Martin and David A. Johnson, asking children to listen for answers to the four questions below.
1. What is the name of the island?
2. What lives there?
3. What grows there?
4. What's the weather?

 Are they able to extract these details as they hear descriptions of Sand Island? Brainstorm possible landscapes and names for the children's own islands. It works well to prepare a sheet of the questions above for each student.

Day 6:

Symbols and keys. Look at the map and chart collection and draw attention to the symbols. Talk about what these little drawings mean and introduce the word "symbol." Then find the map key and talk about how it helps us decode the symbols. Brainstorm and draw some symbols for mountains, rivers, towns, etc. on the board. Give the students scrap paper to practice drawing possible symbols and potential landmarks for their maps, then have them add the ones they want to use and draw keys. Ours loved adorning their maps with cliffs, caves, dragon lairs, coconut groves, fairy villages, and marine monsters. By the end of the lesson, many kids will be aching to share about their islands. Allow extra time for this.

Map-making practice should include discussion of what's important to put on a map. What are the things to notice that will help travelers find their way? Be prepared to introduce the term landmark, and engage children in thinking of various landmarks that let them know they're getting close to school or home.

Day 7:
Coordinate grids. Examine a tourist map or a simple atlas and show the kids how a grid helps people find landmarks more easily. (Arbor children have had previous experience with coordinates during math games.) Have students take turns laying the tracing paper grids you have prepared over their maps and recording the location of important landmarks using the coordinates. Announce that they will all have the chance to travel to their islands, so they'll be able to navigate to these landmarks themselves.

Day 8:
Prepare packing lists: Considering the weather conditions on their islands and their planned activities during the visit, children should write a packing list of supplies they will need.

Evaluate writing mechanics. Making a list is a good chance to practice aligning words on the page, spacing between letters, sounding out words they may not have written before, etc. List-writing is particularly accessible to kindergartners.

Day 9:
The Adventure Store. Each traveler is given $10 to spend at the store and must calculate how best to use it to procure the items on his or her packing list. This is a small-group activity: students can take turns to play store employees serving the travelers; they will receive as much math practice as the customers while they add up the items to be sold. We used a puppet theater as our storefront.

Can they manipulate items to make different combinations of 10? How strong is their number sense? Can the employees check the customers' addition?

Day 10:
Farewell. Students draw and write a farewell postcard to a friend or family member explaining where they're going and when they will return. The class packs a suitcase with their imaginary supplies. A local dignitary (Director Kit Hawkins, in Arbor's case) visits to wish them safe travels. They physically leave the classroom, dispersing onto the playing fields to act out their journeys.

Behind the Scenes, Day 7:
Prepare some simple grid overlays on tracing paper or transparencies to the dimensions of the kids' maps. Label boxes A, B, C along the horizontal axis and 1, 2, 3 along the vertical axis. You may wish to create a simple worksheet asking questions like, "What is in B4?" that students can complete according to their own maps.

Behind the Scenes, Day 9:
Review children's packing lists and prepare an Adventure Store pricelist. Keep the items cheap and make sure there are many combinations that will add up to $10.

Materials, Day 10:
- A suitcase
- Heavy paper cut to 5.5" x 8.5" for postcards

A postcard from Dragonworld

JOURNEYS

Days 11-14:

Adventure writing. Students write journal entries describing their voyage and experiences. We broke down the entries as follows, and offered prompts in our group circle before the children sat down to write:

1. Travel and arriving: *How did you travel to your island? By boat, plane, dragon, fairy chariot? Were you tired when you arrived, or eager to explore?*
2. Landscape and weather: *What does your island's landscape look like? Was it sunny and warm? Stormy? Cold?*
3. A danger and a solution: *Did you meet any people or animals who live on the island? What happened to you that was exciting/scary/challenging, and what did you do?*
4. Return home: *How did you get home? What did you do first, and who were you happy to see? What will you remember about your trip?*

 This is another opportunity to look at writing mechanics, and at imaginative content. Have students adopted elements of any of the journeys in the read-aloud books, or is their adventure entirely new?

Culminating day:

This year we combined a Welcome Home celebration with our H2O Expo, the culminating event for the Primaries' simultaneous science work studying the properties of water and things that float. The children presented their work to their visiting parents and were thrilled to read aloud from their journals and to show off their island maps. If it isn't feasible to bring the parents to school, you might consider asking them to write letters welcoming their adventurers home that you can read aloud to the class.

Maps and artwork by Miles, Lola, Katie P., and Eliana.

UNIT 4:
THE *MAYFLOWER* JOURNEY

Unit cover page: Mayflower *family portrait by kindergartners Olive C., Sean B., and Ada G.*

THE *MAYFLOWER* JOURNEY

After returning from our imaginary journeys, we look at a case study of a real journey from history. The story of the *Mayflower* (pared down to age-appropriate simplicity) is satisfyingly consistent with the stages of a journey we've already introduced and rich with adventure, misadventure, and compelling characters. Many of our children have never before studied a historical event, so we need to begin by articulating the concept of "history." Throughout this study, children's wobbly understanding of the scale of time is evident. For some Primaries, even the idea of a time other than now is a little hazy. *Where does the* Mayflower *voyage of 1620 fall in relation to the dinosaurs? Are the* Mayflower *passengers very old now?* This unit helps them begin to build and calibrate a framework in which to place other historical events. Similarly, the idea of historical research is new. Thinking about evidence and mysteries is intrinsically engaging and leads us to big questions about how we can know what the past was really like.

The easiest path into history is through costume and play. We put Puritan bonnets in the dress-up box, and children are soon tending to a pregnant Elizabeth Hopkins or retrieving John Howland from his plunge overboard. Games of Puritan Tag are invented on the playground. The curriculum feeds play and play feeds enthusiasm for the curriculum.

ESSENTIAL QUESTIONS

- What is history?

- How can we know what happened in the past?

- How do you know if a detail is important?

- What would it be like to undertake a very long journey to a new home?

- Why did the *Mayflower* passengers make such a difficult journey?

- What features of the *Mayflower* allowed the ship to make such a long journey?

- What did the passengers eat, wear, and do to pass the time?

- How did the sailors navigate?

- What does it feel like to act, think, write, and play like a passenger on the *Mayflower*?

- How is life the same today and how has it changed since 1620?

UNIT AIMS

During *Mayflower* studies, students will:

General Habits
- Imagine a time other than now
- Imagine someone else's perspective by role-playing
- Connect with classmates
- Play

Research Skills
- Encounter historical research as a concept
- Practice differentiating between important and trivial information
- Learn strategies for navigating nonfiction books
- Build understanding of a different time period

Reading & Writing Skills
- Enjoy history as a story
- Read nonfiction
- Cement new vocabulary and spatial awareness by labeling diagrams and "nonfiction drawings"
- Write in a character's voice (*Mayflower* journals)
- Apply new knowledge of historical details to add color and specificity to writing

Math & Science Skills	Use numbers as descriptors—of length, distance, time, etc.
	Solve mathematical story problems involving addition and subtraction
	Use a Venn diagram to sort objects by their time periods
	Use number lines to solve problems and explore negative numbers
	Measure out real dimensions of the *Mayflower* to gain a better sense of its scale
	Use tallies to record information and make groups of ten
	Identify some constellations and stars important to navigation
	Explore tools used for celestial navigation
Design Skills	Make diagrams and cross-section drawings
	Learn finger knitting
	Make game boards for Nine Men's Morris
Other Skills	Freely explore dramatic play materials
	Learn the anatomy of a ship
	Taste cuisine and play games from another time

DEEPENING KNOWLEDGE AND HONING SKILLS

What is history? Many children recognize the term as something that happened a long, long time ago. Further discussion refines the idea: yesterday is now history, too. The Primaries contribute a moment in history—dinosaurs, the *Titanic*, the Oregon Trail, the Big Bang, when our great-grandparents were alive—and then we try to put their illustrations in chronological order. This guides us into our study of the *Mayflower's* voyage almost 400 years ago. *What did the travelers on board carry with them? What did they eat? What did the children do for fun? Why did they make such a dangerous journey?*

To find out, we become those travelers, assigning each student a historical character to inhabit during the unit. We paint "self" portraits and write in our journals to record our nervous excitement about the journey, our seasickness, our fear during a big storm, the dramatic rescue of John Howland when he fell overboard, the birth of Oceanus, our joy and relief upon sighting land. Of course, the voyage of the Mayflower provides opportunities to solve math problems too. The list of provisions on board a historical boat of similar size provide fodder for counting and calculating: *If each barrel holds 10 fish, how many barrels are needed for 55 fish? How long will 96 candles last if they burn 5 a day? The Mayflower had three masts. How many masts would there be in a fleet of 3 boats like the Mayflower? In a fleet of 8?* Children use a variety of strategies to solve the problems including math drawings, number lines, and T- charts. We learn that the passengers on board the boat had a limited diet and we conduct a taste test to see if we prefer hardtack, cheese, or dried fruit, charting our preferences on bar graphs. We learn the strategy game Nine Men's Morris and practice finger knitting to simulate the pastimes of the voyagers. In Design, we make pen drawings of ships for a class calendar and collaborate on a mural of the *Mayflower* in cross-section. One year, we recreated the experience of the 'tween decks, taping out dimensions on the Arena floor and borrowing older students at Assembly to hold rods and draped fabric that simulated the low ceiling.

Pulling together as Pilgrims gives us plenty of time to practice being helpful and generous to one another in real life, too. Learning about what groups of people can accomplish in dreaming the same dream and working hard together to achieve it is inspiring for our classroom community.

Mayflower math: the Primary Den's collaborative representation of the provisions on board

Writing as Record-Keeping: Writing Has Purpose

"We were not a little joyful." So wrote William Bradford in his journal upon sighting land after 66 harrowing days aboard the Mayflower. The year offers the discovery of many such jewels that people have written in records of their journeys. *My Father's Dragon*, with adventures and misadventure with tigers and lions with braided manes, neatly illustrated by maps, is a record of a journey. We show the children examples of our own journals from journeys we have taken, our writing recording what the weather was, what we ate, and the funny and strange encounters that travel provides.

All of this demonstrates the purposefulness of writing, inspiring our young writers to try their hand at it, to practice the art of writing regularly. By the time we study the *Mayflower*, the Primaries have had some journaling practice in the form of Weekend News, a Monday morning report of their weekend activities. Now they get to taste historical fiction, using a daily log to imagine the sickening tosses and turns of life on the Mayflower and their character's feelings about this life-altering journey.

Glimpsing the power and various purposes of writing helps to propel Primary writers through the struggles of learning the mechanics of written language.

Problem-Solving: What to Do When Something Goes Wrong

"Good times is good times and bad times is good stories." Inevitably, things go wrong on a journey. The boat capsizes, the weather takes a turn for the worse, and on a whale-watch trip, the whales are a no-show. What do you do then? Learning from models of flexibility, resourcefulness, and turning a bad experience into a good story are important lessons on resilience and perseverance. When a beam on the *Mayflower* broke, resourceful passengers and crew members used a giant jack intended for house construction to temporarily repair and save the ship. So too the children rework their Junk Box designs when their boat fails to float. They scratch their heads as they first identify the problem and work to solve it, trying iterative solutions until they are satisfied. The same set of skills is employed when something goes wrong at recess—identify and articulate the problem, explore some possible solutions, and try it again.

ASSESSMENT AND EVIDENCE

Primary *Mayflower* journals are extraordinarily valuable documents. They show us a great deal more than developments in letter formation and conventional use of punctuation. Under the lens of character education, these journals reveal children's ability to imagine someone else's experience—an ability that is not necessarily inborn and must be cultivated in the name of resolving disputes at recess, finding ways to work together on projects, and a hundred other little skills and attitudes that support human beings in becoming empathetic and moral actors in the world. At the same time, we see children finding ways to color the story according to their own lights, which tells us more about their personalities.

Will was cast as Miles Standish and he took his role of soldier and protector of the colonists seriously. He wrote in his journal, "Land ho! I was ready to kill a bad guy to protect the ship." But another entry revealed an overlay of his own native sweetness: "I was feeling seasick but my heart burst with joy. Oceanus was born!"

Ada, a dyed-in-the-wool animal lover, wrote about finding a kitten on the docks just before the *Mayflower* sailed. Always attentive to matters of form and rectitude, she made sure to apprise the captain of the situation and seek his permission—*after* bringing the cat aboard.

We watch students' interactions when they're in character and observe ample evidence of consideration and flexibility. Rowan spent the better part of one morning's Choice time tending the babydoll Oceanus, his son on our fictional voyage. When a teacher offered that he didn't really have to care for the baby all the time, Rowan calmly explained that Phina—or Elizabeth Hopkins, his wife on the *Mayflower*—had asked him to babysit while she played, and really he didn't mind. He spent the rest of the time practicing his knot-tying skills next to the cradle.

The following pages are from a journal by Henry, an enthusiastic kindergartner whose nascent writing skills are far outpaced by his intellect. By taking dictation, we allow him to fully express his thoughts and understandings.

He lets me into his quarters. I am going to the New World with Rose Standish my wife.

I am finger knitting my own lovely scarf. After this I am going to knit my socks, my gloves, my mitts, and my hat. After that I'm going up to the deck to drink beer and have some porridge. Me and the captain are going on a date night and Rose Standish is going on a date night with Alice Mullins. We're going out at 5:30 to go to the captains quarters to have dinner. He hired a chef to make our dinner.

JOURNEYS

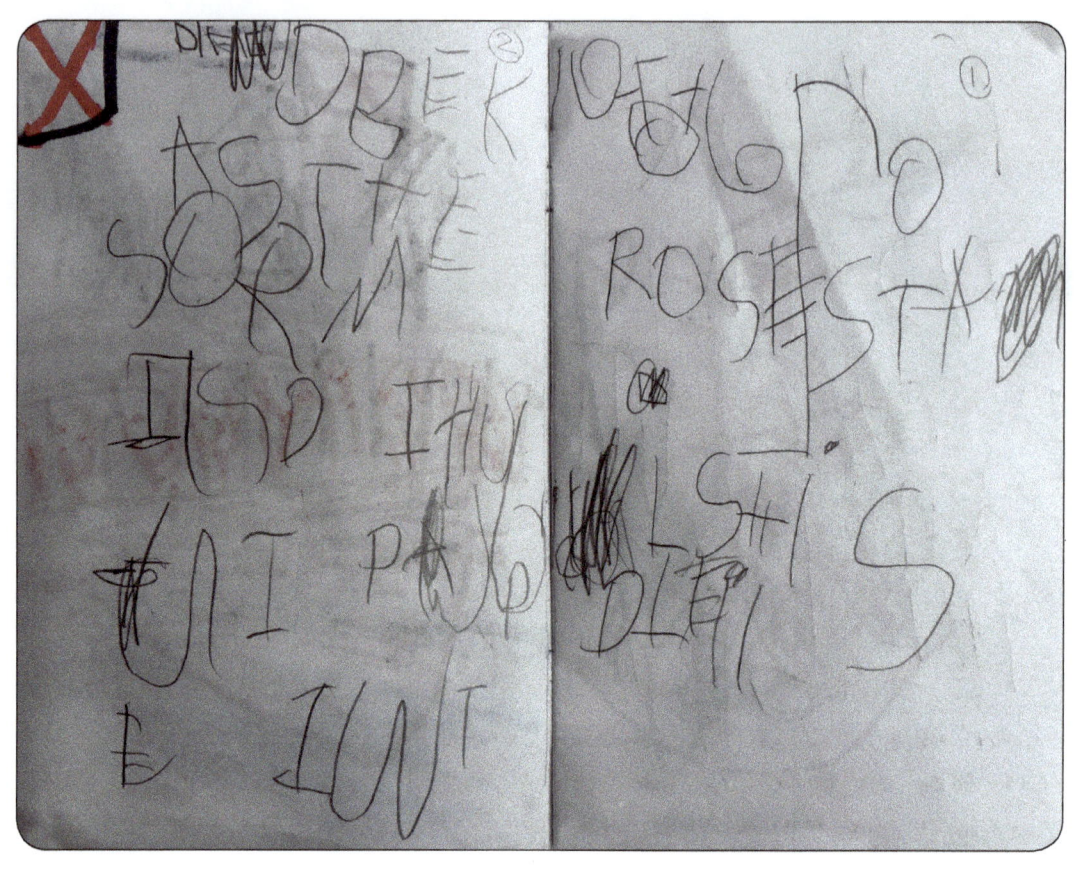

After that I helped John Howland get back on board. He was soaked. I gave him a towel.

1650

I just got a new puppy. The Captain let me have it for free. Elizabeth Hopkins came and showed me the baby. He was a tiny crawling eggshell. The baby had brown eyes like me. His eyes were like marigolds. Every day she brought him to me and Oceanus liked Biscuit the dog. The Captain letted me have a picture of Biscuit, he kept Biscuit in his quarters and gave me pictures. Biscuit is cute! It's very stormy.

16-1051

I'm fixing up the boat. It got tossed around in the storm. I am on land! Biscuit is sniffing my pants because he wants attention. He goes running and chases Wrestling and they run and run and run and chase and chase and chase for a long time. I miss Rose. I was looking for a house for me and Biscuit. I couldn't find one so I built one.

JOURNEYS

What stands out to us about this journal is Henry's strong voice and sense of story. His second entry reflects his friendly nature—on Day 9 he's already making dinner plans with the captain—and incorporates what he understands of grown-up life as he tries to put himself into character. He has an intriguing flair for poetry, too: the new baby Oceanus is "a tiny crawling eggshell" and has "eyes like marigolds."

In the narrative, we notice the addition of a pet dog whose presence on the journey provides all sorts of good tales. Henry even brought a stuffed toy from home to play with on our model ship and to sit by his side while he wrote. Several other Primaries also took the liberty of bringing a pet into the story, which helped them find a way to be on board the ship when they were having trouble imagining what life might be like.

This activity also showed Henry's independence; he began a few entries and spent lots of time adding illustrations to flesh out his ideas rather than waiting for a teacher to be available to write for him.

If the Mayflower passengers used 5 candles each day, how long would a supply of 45 candles last? Laney used math drawings to clearly articulate her thinking. Her solution is age appropriate, clearly communicated, and shows her strong concrete understanding of numbers. Story problems like this one are easily adapted for newer or more experienced mathematicians by adjusting the numbers involved and give students practice at extracting key numerical information, considering the relationships between numbers, and selecting an appropriate operation to arrive at a solution. An Old Hand might solve this kind of problem by using tally marks or repeated addition with numerals rather than math drawings.

BIBLIOGRAPHY

Nonfiction:

Atwood, W.F. *The pilgrim story*. Plymouth, MA: The Memorial Press, 1940.

Carter, E.J. T*he Mayflower compact*. Chicago, IL: Heinemann Library, 2004.

Daugherty, James. *The landing of the pilgrims*. New York, NY: Random House, 1950/1978.

Edwards, Cecil Pepin. *John Alden, steadfast pilgrim*. Boston, MA: Houghton Mifflin, 1965.

George, Jean Craighead. *The first Thanksgiving*. New York,NY: Philomel Books, 1993.

Grace, Catherine, O'Neill. *1621: a new look at Thanksgiving*. Washington, DC: National Geographic Society, 2001.

Leacock, Elspeth. *Journeys in time, a new atlas of American history*. New York: Houghton Mifflin, 2001.

Mayflower 1620: a new look at a pilgrim voyage. Washington, DC: National Geographic Society, 2003.

McGovern, Ann. *The Mayflower in 1620, if you sailed on*. New York: Scholastic, 1969/1991.
  This question book is a favorite.

Penner, Lucille Recht. *Eating the plates: a pilgrim book of food and manners*. New York: Macmillan, 1991.

Philbrick, Nathaniel. *Mayflower: a story of courage, community, and war*. New York, NY: Penguin Books, 2006.

San Souci, Robert. *N.C. Wyeth's pilgrims*. San Francisco, CA: Chronicle, 1991.

Sewell, Marcia. *Thunder from the clear sky*. New York, NY: Antheneum Books, 1995.

Waters, Kate. *On the Mayflower*. New York, NY: Scholastic, 1996.
  Kate Waters's books are truly excellent resources.

Waters, Kate. *Richard Eaton's day: a day in the life of a pilgrim boy*. New York, NY: Scholastic, 1993.

Waters, Kate. *Samuel Eaton's day*. New York, NY: Scholastic, 1993.

Waters, Kate. *Sarah Morton's day, a day in the life of a pilgrim girl*. New York, NY: Scholastic, 1989.

Waters, Kate. *Tapenum's day, a Wampanoaq indian boy in pilgrim times*. New York, NY: Scholastic, 1996.

Picture Books:

Bunting, Eve. *How many days to America?: a Thanksgiving story*. New York, NY: Clarion Books, 1988.

Bunting, Eve. *A turkey for Thanksgiving*. New York, NY: Clarion Books, 1990.

Fiction:

Bowen, Gary. *Stranded at Plimouth Plantation 1626*. New York, NY: Harper Collins, 1993.

Cohen, Barbara. *Molly's pilgrim*. New York, NY: Bantam, 1983.

Dorris, Michael. *Guests*. New York, NY: Hyperion, 1994.

Lasky, Kathryn. *A journey to the new world, the diary of Remember Patience Whipple*. New York, NY: Scholastic, 1995.

Moses and Thatcher play Nine Men's Morris

UNIT 5:
ANIMAL MIGRATIONS

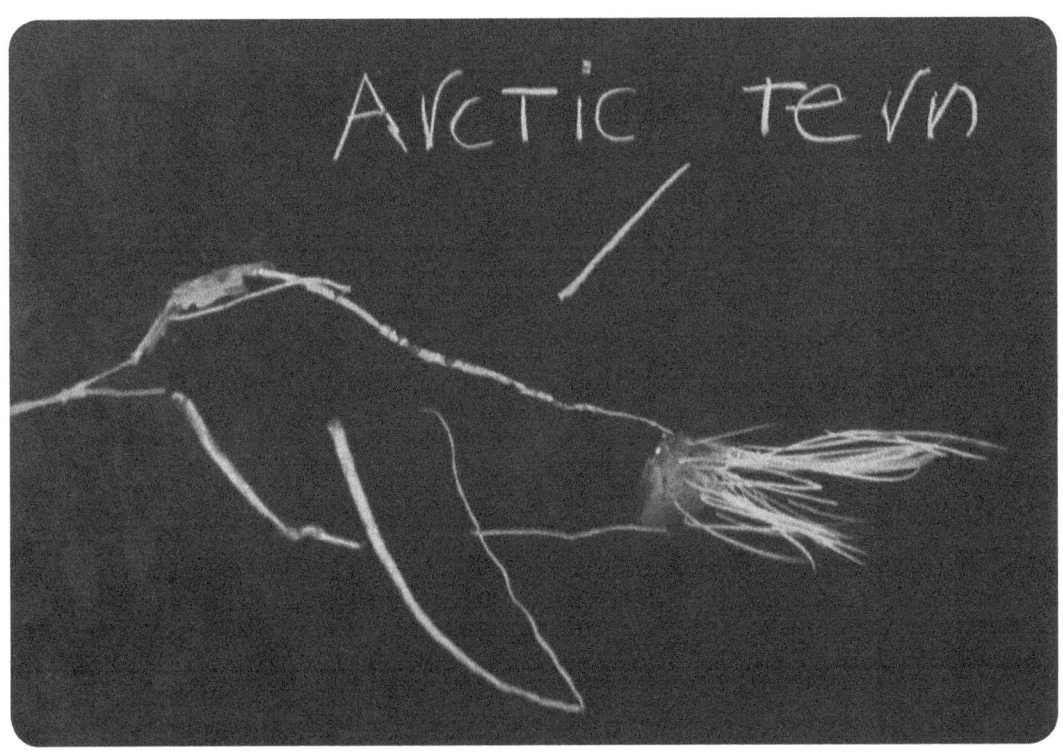

Unit cover page: Primary "nonfiction drawing" of an arctic tern, carefully labeled
At right, Primaries ride the caribou they built in the block area.

ANIMAL MIGRATIONS

People aren't the only ones who make journeys. In this unit, we cast our eyes to the sky, the land and the water to investigate the incredible travels of migrating animals. They don't make packing lists, but they do do some things that look familiar to our now-experienced travelers. Naturally drawn to animals, Primary children are easily captivated by the particular habits and routines of critters. Using salmon, Arctic terns, monarch butterflies, caribou, and humpback whales as case studies, the Primary children have the opportunity to compare and contrast the migrations of these remarkable animals.

Gathering up migration facts takes us deeper into research and the realm of nonfiction. As the Primaries' reading skills develop, they can build independence in their encounters with books. More experienced Old Hands can pair off with early readers to comb our classroom resources for information and everyone can gain skill in honing research questions. Figuring out the right question to ask is the first step in productive inquiry. We talk about "lightning" and "meaty" questions—those that can be satisfied with an easy *yes* or *no* vs. those *how* and *why* questions that require real delving and lead to even more questions.

Migration studies take us to new environments: the frozen tundra, the balmy seas around Hawaii, the mountains of Mexico. Children begin to develop an awareness of the world's various biomes and notice the differences between equatorial and high latitudes. We learn how animal migrations are affected by human actions and patterns of development, too, and we seek to nourish a sense of environmental conservation.

ESSENTIAL QUESTIONS

- What is a migration?
- What are some reasons that animals migrate?
- How do different species navigate?
- How are migrating species similar? How are they different?
- What impact do human beings have on these different migrating animals? On their environment?
- How do we make sense of very large numbers?

UNIT AIMS

During Migrations studies, students will:

General Habits

Wonder at the marvels of the natural world

Develop a sense of environmental conservation

Collaborate on whole-class projects with effort and flexibility

Research Skills

Use nonfiction materials independently, within a group, and guided by a teacher or peer

Distinguish between fiction and nonfiction books

Identify important information

Ask and hone questions to deepen their understanding of animal migrations

Further develop research skills to find specific information within a text

Develop organizational systems to compare data

Create and analyze a group matrix to compare migrating animals

Reading & Writing Skills	Record facts in personal migration books
	Listen to fiction and nonfiction read-alouds
	Attend to story settings
	Restate facts in their own words
Math & Science Skills	Use scale to compare and make sense of the big numbers in migration distances, using Unifix cubes (1 cube = 100 miles)
	Continue to develop strategies for solving math problems, including using T-charts and reading graphs
	Practice concepts of place value, making grouping of ones, tens, hundreds, thousands
	Use maps and globes to trace migration routes
	Gain familiarity with world geography
	Develop awareness of different climates and biomes around the world
	Organize and compare statistics on different animals and their migrations
	Describe the physical features and social structures of the different species that make their migrations possible
	Use microscopes to examine salmon eggs and salmon scales
	Study and compare the life cycles of various animals
Design Skills	Model animals in three dimensions and incorporate scientific knowledge of their habitat to strive toward accurate representation of the environment in a diorama
	Apply new understanding of scale and work carefully with fragile materials to craft an oversize model of a butterfly wing

DEEPENING KNOWLEDGE AND HONING SKILLS

In an initial discussion about migration, we find many children already know that some birds and whales travel south for the winter. Some know that salmon swim out to the ocean and return to the stream they were born in years later. But there are those animals that leave us a little unsure about whether they migrate: Crabs? Robins? Lobsters? As we begin our reading, we start to collect some remarkable facts about champion migrators, such as the Arctic terns that spend eight months a year traveling the 25,000 miles from the North Pole to the South Pole and back again. This is a chance to admire some remarkable critters but also to practice listening for important facts during read-alouds and to begin trying to restate information in our own words. This is a sophisticated skill that our students will hone for years to come. Our job is to provide an introduction, modeling for the group the art of recalling facts, returning to the text for verification, and succinctly restating the information. The group's efforts are recorded by each student in his or her migration booklet.

The journeys of amazing critters provide an opportunity for us to grapple with some very big numbers. We consider place value by grouping Unifix cubes, tens' rods, hundreds' charts, and other manipulatives and practice math drawings. We stack cubes to show the miles that animals travel and compare migration distances on graphs. We make teeny tiny models of imposing caribou and a gigantic model of the delicate wing of a monarch butterfly.

We learn about caribou, which travel in vast herds that can spread over 200 miles, and salmon that swim out to sea and then return to spawn in the very creek where they were born. We practice diagrams as "nonfiction drawings," working as a class and then individually to draw and label the parts of a salmon's body. Children assemble and paint life-size stuffed paper salmon, and in Science they have the opportunity to examine salmon roe and skin under a microscope. We also learn about monarch butterflies, which migrate more than 1,000 miles to return to the birthplace of their forebears.

Meanwhile, we get to know the birds that visit our campus, luring them in for closer observation with treats of "birdy bagels" and birdseed-stuffed orange halves. We gather data about our visitors and consider the factors that might be affecting our results.

Nonfiction: Identifying Important Facts and Finding Evidence

A first grader announces, after completing her job of straightening the bookshelves, "The nonfiction looks good, but the fiction books were a little messy." What do these genres mean to a six-year-old? She knows that fiction is "made up" and nonfiction is "true." She can place *Mr. Putter and Tabby* in its proper spot and identifies *The Life Cycle of a Monarch* as a book of nonfiction. She might readily take up either of these titles, but how will the reading experience differ?

Through nonfiction read-alouds, we model the practice of identifying important facts and finding evidence. We ask the children to raise a pinky (letter "i" in the manual alphabet) when they hear us read an important fact. When those pinkies go up and stay up for the duration of the book, we talk about the difference between key facts and those that are fascinating but non-essential. During our study of whales the Primaries have ample opportunity to think about these distinctions. It is not an easy task to simultaneously listen to information and analyze whether each fact is essential knowledge.

Primaries are learning that there are ways to discover truths about their world beyond asking the nearest grown-up. *How do sperm whales sleep? What do humpback whales eat? How tall is a male orca's dorsal fin?* We read through books together and look for answers and evidence. We wonder aloud about how a baby whale is born and flip back in the book to where we remember reading about the nurseries in Mexico, pointing to the illustration or the written passage. We learn about the index and table of contents and talk about alphabetical order. The children see the utility in these navigational aids and begin to explore them on their own. Soon the whale books on the shelf are filled with sticky notes, each yellow tab pointing to evidence and important information: "I found this picture of a sperm whale and it's upside down and guess what, it's sleeping!" "This book has a lot, I mean a lot, of things about orcas. It says that their dorsal fins are six feet tall!"

ASSESSMENT AND EVIDENCE

Each student selected a particular salmon to recreate from a poster of various species and subspecies in different phases of life. We drew the body outlines (two per child) and encouraged the students to mix paints to just the right hues to capture these colorful creatures. We stapled the two sides of each fish together, stuffed them with newspaper, and hung a whole school of migrating salmon from our ceiling.

Laney's caribou diagram is exceptional—accurate beyond her years, with careful attention to the articulation of the leg joints and shape of the head. Each body part is clearly labeled.

The whole class collaborates on a pair of tissue paper butterfly wings at exploded scale. The tissue paper squares are glued down to a sheet of clear plastic film. We recommend mapping out the black vein structures first and then filling in the spaces with color. This year the Primary Nest class went for a realistic, teacher-guided structure, while the Primary Den children worked out their own interpretations. Below, a flock of monarchs made independently by students traces the route to and from Mexico.

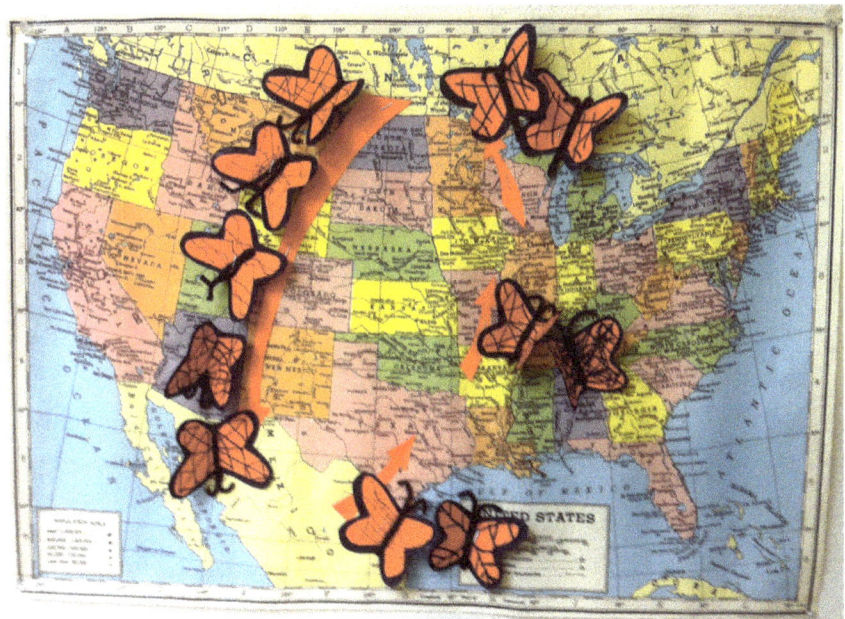

In studying arctic terns, we read aloud and practiced listening for important facts. As a class, we restated those facts we remembered at the end of the reading and the teachers recorded them on a large sheet of chart paper. The students selected a few facts to transfer to their Migration books. Edie, a first grader, is clearly comfortable copying facts. Her handwriting is neat and careful, with consistent spacing. Although she has included a few superfluous periods, her work shows her awareness of punctuation and capitalization. Next steps for Edie and her classmates include generating fact recall more independently—in the Greek unit, for example, we will ask the children, "Are there any other interesting facts you remember that you'd like to add to your book?"

BIBLIOGRAPHY

Picture Books:

Gill, Shelley. *Swimmer*. Seattle, WA: Sasquatch Books, 1995.

O'Flatharta, Antoine. *Hurry and the monarch*. New York, NY: Knopf, 2005.

Swope, Sam. *Gotta go! Gotta go!* New York, NY: Square Fish, 2000.
Really fun.

Nonfiction:

Bancroft, Henrietta. *Animals in winter*. New York, NY: Harper Collins, 1987.

Berks, Marianne. *Going home: the mystery of animal migration*. Nevada City, CA: Dawn Publications, 2010.

Carney, Elizabeth. *Great migrations: whales, wildebeests, butterflies, elephants, and other amazing animals on the move*. Washington, D.C.: National Geographic, 2010.
A flashy title with lots of pictures and tantalizing glimpses of species we don't study in depth.

Catt, Thessaly. *Migrating with the arctic tern*. New York, NY: Rosen Publishing Group, 2011.

Catt, Thessaly. *Migrating with the caribou*. New York, NY: Rosen Publishing Group, 2011.

Catt, Thessaly. *Migrating with the humpback whale*. New York, NY: Rosen Publishing Group, 2011.

Catt, Thessaly. *Migrating with the monarch butterfly*. New York, NY: Rosen Publishing Group, 2011.

Catt, Thessaly. *Migrating with the salmon*. New York, NY: Rosen Publishing Group, 2011.

Cherry, Lynne. *Flute's journey*. New York, NY: Harcourt, 1987.

Cohn, Scotti. *On the move, mass migrations*. Mt. Pleasant, SC: Sylvan Dell, 2013

Dowson, Nick. *North: the amazing story of Arctic migration*. Somerville, MA: Candlewick, 2011.

Edwards, Roberta. *Flight of the butterflies*. New York, NY: Penguin Young Readers, 2010.

Frost, Helen. *Caribou*. Mankato, MN: Capstone Press, 2007.

Frost, Helen. *Monarch and milkweed*. New York, NY: Atheneum Books for Young Readers, 2008.

Gans, Roma. *How do birds find their way?* New York, NY: Harper Collins, 1996.

Gibbons, Gail. *Monarch butterflies*. New York, NY: Holiday House, 1991.
Gail Gibbons is a fantastic Primary-level science writer. We have a shelf devoted to her works in the classroom.

Himmelman, John. *A monarch butterfly's life*. New York, NY: Children's Press, 1993.

Kostyal, K.M. *Great migrations: official companion to the National Geographic channel global television event*. Washington, D.C.: National Geographic, 2010.

Lasky, Kathryn. *Monarchs*. New York, NY: Gulliver Books Paperbacks, 1993.

Nelson, Robin. *Migration*. Minneapolis, MN: Lerner Publications Company, 2011.

Pyle, Robert Michael. *Chasing monarchs: migrating with the butterflies of passage*. Boston, MA: Houghton Mifflin, 1999.

Rylant, Cynthia. *The journey: stories of migration*. New York, NY: Scholastic, 2006. *A must-have*.

Simon, Seymour. *They swim the seas: the mystery of animal migration*. San Diego, CA: Harcourt Brace & Co., 1998.

Urquhart, Jennifer C. *Animals that travel*. Washington, D.C.: National Geographic, 1982.

UNIT 6:
WHALES

Unit cover page: whale card by Ella B.

WHALES

Knowing some facts about animal migration, the children are now ready to study a champion migrator in depth. Children are avid collectors of facts, ready to stuff their pockets full of statistics and trivia. Whales offer a wealth of new vocabulary for children to collect: pectoral fins, dorsal fins, flukes and blowholes, gulpers and gunkers. Field guides are practical and enticing resources for investigating favorite species: bottlenose dolphins, belugas, narwhals. As fellow mammals, our Primaries can relate to belly buttons, nursing babies, and strong family connections. Whales' underwater world, though, forces us to wonder how it all works for them. *How does a calf nurse? How do whales sleep? How do they know their mother?* A whale's sheer length and girth inspires a sense of wonder at these mighty animals' power and strength—particularly captivating qualities to the small and seemingly vulnerable Primary child.

ESSENTIAL QUESTIONS

- What is a mammal?

- What are some distinguishing features of different types of whales?

- Why do whales migrate?

- How can we use maps to track the migratory pattern of a certain whale?

- What is the human impact on whales and their environment?

- What is a scale model?

- How can we make sense of whales' enormous size?

- What is an important fact?

- What tools do nonfiction books offer to aid us in doing research?

UNIT AIMS

During Whales studies, students will:

General Habits

Wonder at the similarities and differences between mammals

Develop a sense of agency in contributing to good stewardship of our planet

Research Skills

Learn to use a Know/Wonder/Learn chart to guide the search for information

Hone their ability to ask good questions

Listen attentively during nonfiction read-alouds

Distinguish between important and non-essential facts

Compare and contrast data

Show increased independence in gathering information

Practice using the index and table of contents in nonfiction books to locate specific information

Restate facts in their own words

Use matrices to sort and classify information

Use tools similar to those used by researchers (binoculars, diagrams, whale identification charts, compass, maps/charts)

Reading & Writing Skills

Navigate a library of material about whales

Record specific information on whale fact cards (name, type, length, what they eat, where they migrate)

Practice handwriting

Practice writing conventions (punctuation, capitalization)

Math & Science Skills

Measure with standard, non-standard, and metric units

Solve mathematical word problems

Solve math problems involving scale, using Unifix cubes to represent various units of measure

Graph data, including length of whales and duration of dives

Hone understanding of time (How long is a minute?)

Compare large numbers (migration distances)

Practice classification (how various whales eat, why they migrate, size)

Consider features and systems that are common to all mammals

Use microscopes

Make scientific drawings based on observations through the microscope

Understand neutral buoyancy and practice iterative design to achieve it with plankton models

Experiment with echolocation using tuning forks in water

Design Skills

Practice observational drawing

Creatively use recycled materials to construct "scientific equipment" for play

Build models (teeth, baleen, fins, whole whales) using a variety of media

DEEPENING KNOWLEDGE AND HONING SKILLS

Gray whales migrate farther than any other cetacean—6,000 miles—and pass by Oregon's coast in the process. Researchers identify individual orcas by their dorsal fins and saddle markings. A sperm whale can hold its breath for 90 minutes. Our whale books quickly fill with all kinds of fascinating facts as we continue to practice the habits of gathering and recording information. Having had some practice at elementary research in our study of migrating animals, the children are growing increasingly skilled and habituated to listen for important facts. While most of the work recording facts is still done as a group, some children are inspired to add "extra" facts, restating information in their own words with developing independence. There is ample opportunity to discuss their reasoning and practice citing evidence: "I think that's important because…"

Studying whales creates rich opportunities in Science: we view plankton and krill under the microscope, making observational drawings of the tiny creatures the great whales consume in staggering quantities—humpbacks eat as much as 5,500 pounds of plankton a day during the summer when they're in cold waters. We learn how baleen whales gulp mouthfuls of water and push it back out with their tongues to strain the plankton with their baleen. We give it a try with vegetable soup! We listen to a variety of whale clicks and songs and experience how a "blubber glove" filled with vegetable shortening keeps your hand surprisingly comfortable in a tub of icy water.

Comparing various whales lets us engage in explorations of scale, modeling a life-size male orca dorsal fin (6 feet), carefully measuring and creating a stuffed paper humpback at 1 : 4 scale so it can fit in our classroom, drawing a matrix to easily contrast humpback and orca statistics. Accurately using a ruler is an important math skill for Primaries, so we practice measuring classroom objects the same size as an orca tooth—12 cm—lining up the 0 with care and discussing centimeters vs. inches. In a grand finale of scale modeling, we fill the Arena with a full-size gray whale, built by parents from plastic bags and inflated with fans, with entry flaps so that students can walk right inside the leviathan.

Each year, we invite a friend who spent a summer in the San Juan Islands taking inventory of the resident orcas. After learning about her duties and the equipment she used, we transform the block area into a whale lab, building computer screens from cardboard boxes and fashioning hydrophones in the Junk Box. Using toilet paper tube binoculars, the children sight orcas and, like scientists, busily record their findings on a clipboard.

Museums & Bake Sales: Curate & Present to an Authentic Audience

Many units in the lower grades at Arbor culminate in a celebration of learning to which we invite parents, grandparents, and siblings. We often choose to display evidence of our hard work in the form of a class hands-on museum, with each child putting forth extra effort to prepare his written pieces and design projects for an outside audience. Thinking about leading visitors on a guided tour of all we've learned brings each child back into contact with every aspect of our studies, cementing new knowledge. The "tour guides" brim with importance as they show their parents around, relishing the role of "expert" and practicing the art of hospitality as they share their school world with their parents.

Our Migration Museum, presented at the end of our Whales focus, is a fine example. We display beautifully illustrated accordion books of migrating animal facts, sewn models of plankton, krill sculptures, life-size baleen models, whale fact cards, and more. We set up hands-on experiments for parents to try: they can discover the insulating effects of the "blubber glove," build a model of plankton that neither sinks nor floats but hovers, or construct a representation of whale lengths with math manipulatives. In preparation for our visitors, the children undertake a serious company-is-coming cleaning of the classroom: "I'm going to make it all sparkly and golden," announces a boy with a broom. Primaries are rightly proud to show off their hard work and gratified by the visitors' approval. "I saw my dad's face turn from curious about migration to excited and proud of me when he looked at my migration book," one boy reflected afterward.

Our learning is also made public in the ever-popular whale-themed bake sale we hold to raise money for the protection of whales and their habitat. A presentation by a recent Arbor graduate who did her Senior Project on ocean health was particularly galvanizing for our young activists, and we undertook a public service announcement campaign to educate our customers: Use Less Plastic!

ASSESSMENT AND EVIDENCE

Addie's whale card, as well as being beautiful, is evidence of this first grader's careful observation of a gray whale's baleen, barnacles, and relatively small dorsal fin.

> Name ILSA
>
> Orca teeth are about 3 inches long.
> Find some things in the classroom that are:
>
> | SHORTER THAN AN ORCA TOOTH | ABOUT THE SAME | LONGER THAN AN ORCA TOOTH |
> |---|---|---|
> | TOY ELFIT | TOY PIG NEST SIN | BLOKS DINSR |

This kindergartner's hunt for objects around the classroom is age appropriate, showing invented spelling, evidence of exploration, and ability to record her findings. For children who are just beginning to measure objects, we may give the assignment in inches; Old Hands who can measure with more finesse can tackle working in centimeters. The activity is a good example of how Theme enlivens our work across disciplines; here the aim is to practice using a ruler and build our young students' sense of comparative size.

BIBLIOGRAPHY

Picture Books:

Armour, Michael C., illus. by Katie Lee. *Orca song*. Phoenix, AZ: Futech Interactive Books, 1994.

Fogliano, Julie, illus. by Erin E. Stead. *If you want to see a whale*. New York, NY: Roaring Brook Press, 2013.

Horácek, Petr. *Puffin Peter*. Somerville, MA: Candlewick Press, 2011.

Kimmel, Eric A., illus. by Andrew Glass. *Moby Dick: chasing the great white whale*. New York, NY: MacMillan, 2012.

Kipling, Rudyard. "How the whale got his throat" (in *Just So Stories*). Cambridge, MA: Candlewick Press, 2004.

Lucas, David. *Whale*. New York, NY: Knopf, 2006.

McCloskey, Robert. *Burt Dow, deep water man*. New York, NY: Viking, 1963.

McFarlane, Sheryl, illus. by Ron Lightburn. *Waiting for the whales*. Victoria, BC: Orca Book Publishers, 1991.

Melville, Herman, adapted and illus. by Allan Drummond. *Moby Dick*. New York, NY: Farrar, Straus and Giroux, 1997.

Ryder, Joanne, illus. by Michael Rothman. *Winter whale*. New York, NY: Morrow, 1991.

Rylant, Cynthia. *The whales*. New York, NY: Scholastic, 1996.

Sayre, April Pulley, illus. by Jamie Hogan. *Here come the humpbacks!* Watertown, MA: Charlesbridge, 2013.

Schuch, Steve, illus. by Peter Sylvada. *A symphony of whales*. New York, NY: Harcourt Brace & Co., 1999.

Sís, Peter. *An ocean world*. New York, NY: HarperCollins, 1992.

Van Dusen, Chris. *Down to the sea with Mr. Magee*. San Francisco, CA: Chronicle, 2000.

Nonfiction:

Berger, Gilda. *Whales*. New York, NY: Doubleday, 1987.

Carrick, Carol. *Whaling days*. New York, NY: Clarion, 1993.

The Cousteau Society. *Whales*. New York, NY: Simon & Schuster, 1993.

Davies, Nicola. *Big blue whale*. Somerville, MA: Candlewick Press, 1997.

Flaherty, Chuck. *Whales of the northwest*. Seattle, WA: Cherry Lane Press, 1990.

Gordon, David G. *Field guide to the orca*. Seattle, WA: Sasquatch Books, 1990.

Jeunesse, Gallimard. *Whales*. New York, NY: Scholastic, 1991.

Kalman, Bobbie and Kurana Thal. *The life cycle of a whale*. New York, NY: Crabtree Publishing Company, 2002.

McNulty, Faith. *How whales walked into the sea*. New York, NY: Scholastic, 1999.

Milton, Joyce. *Whales, the gentle giants*. New York, NY: Random House, 1989.

Posonby, David. *The anatomy of the sea*. San Francisco, CA: Chronicle, 2005.

Simon, Seymour. *Whales*. New York, NY: HarperCollins, 1989.

Wells, Robert E. *Is a blue whale the biggest thing there is?* Morton Grove, IL: Albert Whitman & Company, 1993.

Poetry:

Worth, Valerie. *Animal poems*. New York, NY: Farrar, Straus and Giroux, 2007.

UNIT 7:
GREEK MYTHOLOGY

Unit cover page: "The Birth of Aphrodite," Noemi L.'s interpretation of the Renaissance painting by Sandro Botticelli

GREEK MYTHOLOGY

Before there was the world, what was there? The stories humans have invented to explain their own origins are varied and fascinating and allow young children to grapple with big ideas about what is real and what is not real, about forces that are at work in the world, about the power of narrative to serve as a vessel for human hopes and fears. We dip into many traditions, then settle in to focus on the myths told by the ancient Greeks. Mount Olympus provides a rich backdrop for multidimensional characters who entertain us with their outlandish antics. Young children—who are sorting out the give and take of social interactions in how to share, take turns, be kind to one another, and use their words—find respite in the dramatic flair of justifiably jealous Hera, thunderbolt-wielding Zeus, trouble-making Eris, and self-centered Aphrodite. These characters, in all of their immortality and authority, are generous in sharing with us their innumerable flaws.

Traveling all the way back to ancient Greece allows us to expand our understanding of history yet again. You think the *Mayflower* was a long time ago? Wait till you hear about the voyage of Odysseus. Studying one last epic journey, we listen to the tales of his adventures and retell them chronologically. We solve math problems incorporating suitors or sheep, depending on Odysseus's current predicament. We explore the foggy terra incognita where history becomes myth and then add to the complexity of it all by examining modern Greece, where traffic whizzes around the ancient temples and daily life unfolds much as it does for us.

The unit culminates with a student-written play retelling the myth of the Golden Apple. This provides an opportunity for the children to try real stagecraft, a step beyond the happy hours they've spent dressing up during Choice time. We learn to memorize lines, remember cues and placement on stage, project our voices, and practice acting in slow motion. Every child gets to experience how his own small role contributes to a large production. Performing this play for parents and siblings and showing off a Greek museum of shared work also provides the Primaries with an audience for all of their efforts.

ESSENTIAL QUESTIONS

- What is a myth? Is it fact or fiction?

- What are the basic components of a story?

- How are the different Greek gods and goddesses characterized?

- What is a play?

- How does an actor prepare for a play?

- What strategies are helpful for performing in front of an audience?

- What made the ancient Greeks such amazing architects?

- What is it like to live in Greece today?

UNIT AIMS

During Greek Mythology studies, students will:

General Habits

Ask questions

Imagine new possibilities for dramatic play

Contribute to a group working toward a common goal

Practice flexibility and compromise

Research Skills

Identify important facts in nonfiction reading/listening

Organize information to keep track of the many characters in Greek mythology

Develop background knowledge about ancient Greek culture and history

Distinguish between mythical, ancient, and modern life in the country of Greece

Reading & Writing Skills

Write a collaborative creation myth

Write a biography for the play program

Read creation myths from around the world

Identify common themes in creation myths

Consider character traits (as embodied by the Greek gods and goddesses) and how they affect story

Distinguish fact from fiction

Sequence events in retelling stories

Learn the Greek alphabet

Math & Science Skills

Extract numerical information from word problems

Use math drawings to solve story problems involving addition and subtraction

Explore multiplication

Explore area and perimeter using graph paper and height x length notation

Use T-charts to solve math problems

Use tens' rods and unit cubes to solve math problems

Build arrays with Unifix cubes

Identify and define shapes

Use Geoboards and Tangrams to explore geometric relationships

Sift through a small-scale dig site as archaeologists

Design Skills

Apply knowledge of scale and beginning understanding of perspective to draw Greek temples

Shape coiled clay vessels

Illustrate scenes to tell a collective story

Exercise creativity in repurposing Junk Box materials to build props and costumes

Other Skills

Learn basic methods of acting (getting into character, voice projection, memorizing lines, blocking)

Perform for an audience

DEEPENING KNOWLEDGE AND HONING SKILLS

It is our experience that children can manage more ambiguity than adults commonly assume. In fact, they are quite comfortable speculating about what there was before time began. They explain, "There was just a big open space," or "People lived on Mars and then migrated to Earth," or "There were just really big plants."

So they love to hear the creation stories from a variety of cultures. Together we read creation tales from Japan, Africa, and the Arctic. Finally, we read the Greek creation myth, noticing similarities and differences to the other myths we have heard.

Then we begin to make the acquaintance of the most important Greek gods and goddesses. Over several weeks we use *D'Aulaires' Book of Greek Myths* and Aliki's *The Gods and Goddesses of Mt. Olympus* to learn about the whole pantheon, from Aphrodite to Zeus. The children begin to create their own books of the Greek gods, adding a new entry every few days. At this point in the year, they have had a lot of practice distilling important facts, and together we craft a short introduction to each god or goddess.

The characters from Greek mythology come alive in our classrooms: the children don togas made from bedsheets, aspiring Zeuses brandish cardboard lightning bolts, and wise Athena juggles her stuffed owl and her shield. In addition, we construct an enormous model of Mt. Olympus, plant herbs that feature in Greek cookery, and learn some Greek music and dance. The myths themselves inspire conversations about jealousy and selfishness, revenge and arrogance. We look at a number of paintings of the birth of Aphrodite and draw our own renditions; we experiment with perspective drawing to represent the Parthenon and try our hand at building temples in the block area. We look at amphorae and make clay coil pots with large loopy handles. Temples feature in math problems as we began to study area and perimeter, using arrays and graph paper to investigate the building blocks of multiplication. They also serve as a vehicle for beginning studies of perspective—we notice how each step up to the Parthenon is drawn as though it is shorter than the one beneath, and try our hands at mimicking this illusion of three dimensions.

How do we know so much about this culture that flourished thousands of years ago? We talk about the work of archaeologists, their discovery of ancient objects and oh-so-patient efforts to uncover and preserve what they find. We practice brushing sand away from "artifacts" and making hypotheses about their significance. *What kind of person might have jewelled necklaces in her tomb? What period would this column fragment date from?* Our favorite Art Look question, "What do you see that makes you think that?" is a touchstone here.

We read select episodes from the *Odyssey*, meeting our clever (if imperfect) hero, Odysseus, as well as the cast of colorful characters that he encounters along his journey—one-eyed Polyphemus, the Sirens, Circe, and many more. We invite willing parents to re-enact some of these spellbinding stories. The Primaries delight in watching Odysseus's ten-year journey come to life—who could resist watching her dad, almost unrecognizable in his Cyclops costume, or her mom, turned by Circe's magic into a pig? These stories inspire new activities in the classroom: sewing Cyclops eye beanbags, making yogurt cheese flavored with herbs from the garden, and inventing board games that involve twists and turns and narrow passages such as those Odysseus sailed through.

But no Primary Greek study would be complete without a performance of "The Golden Apple" from a script written by long-ago Primaries Myles Buchanan and Leah Thompson in

2000. The story itself invites us to think about what can happen when someone feels excluded and when we insist on distinguishing ourselves at the expense of others. In preparing to take on characters, we talk about the importance of the ensemble, how the performance can only succeed if we all work together. Everyone signs a flexibility contract, agreeing to accept and do his best with the role he is assigned, but teachers take requests into account in the casting. A series of acting workshops ensues, with children practicing "slouder"—slower and louder— line delivery, finding their places, slow-motion food fighting, listening for cues, and (hardest of all) waiting patiently backstage. Everyone memorizes lines and we orchestrate musical accompaniment. We make sets, programs and posters, tickets and invitations. Parents help by making costumes at home—though a few enterprising Primaries have undertaken to sew their own togas—and preparing a potluck Greek feast for all to enjoy after the performance. The play is always a joyous success, with older students finding reasons to linger near the Amphitheater for a glimpse of the action and a moment of nostalgia for the time when they portrayed Hephaestus or Helen. It's also an important bonding moment for the class, with everyone pitching in to make the event as wonderful as possible.

The performance is part of a larger Greek Celebration, a triumphant sharing of work as the students tour their families around the classroom. Using a class-made checklist as a guide, each child proudly shares his Greek gods and goddesses book, Greek math, and creation story. Parents get to view a wall of self-portraits, hand-drawn Greek flags, the results of the olive taste test, and prove their knowledge of Greek trivia at the Question Board. Table tops display the children's clay vessels, different styles of Greek columns made from clay, a model of Mount Olympus populated with clothespin deities. Families are invited to try on Greek costumes, draw a Greek flag, and leaf through our library of Greek books.

Max B. serenades the "Golden Apple" audience with Greek tunes on his violin

Distinguishing Fact from Fiction

To Primaries, the line between fact and fiction can be fuzzy. They toggle between the real and the imaginary all day long. It is perfectly normal to be a dog during a recess game and, ten minutes later, to be working on backward fives while filling in the date on the calendar; to spend Choice time as Athena, an owl perched on your shoulder as you evade Zeus's thunderbolts, then settle down to write about your weekend of riding your new red bike.

While looking through a book of actors portraying life in Plimoth Plantation, a student once asked, "How old are they now?" Even after an explanation of the replica ship and living history actors, confusion lingered in his eyes. He understood that the *Mayflower* was a real ship that had sailed almost four hundred years ago, but seeing photographs of Pilgrims about their daily business was perplexing.

This is not uncommon among Primaries; the question "Wait, is this real?" is often heard as we move through our days. The unit on ancient Greece steeps us in both fact and fiction, and allows the Primaries practice at distinguishing between them. While studying the Greek gods and goddesses, we talk about ancient belief systems and also about the modern country of Greece. We spend time locating Greece on a map, look at photographs of a colleague's trip to Greece, and draw the Greek flag. Grounded in this factual place, we can also role-play the drama on Mount Olympus—how Demeter causes the seasons and Zeus the thunderstorms, how mischievous Eros's arrows cause unsuspecting passersby to fall in love.

Similarly, the Greek mythology unit provides an opportunity to get comfortable with the idea that people hold different beliefs to explain the mysteries of life. It is never too early to develop an appreciation for comparative world views and building a vocabulary that embraces diversity of thought and belief. "Some people believe…"

ASSESSMENT AND EVIDENCE

Illustrations of the Greek creation myth by Simon N. and Simon B.

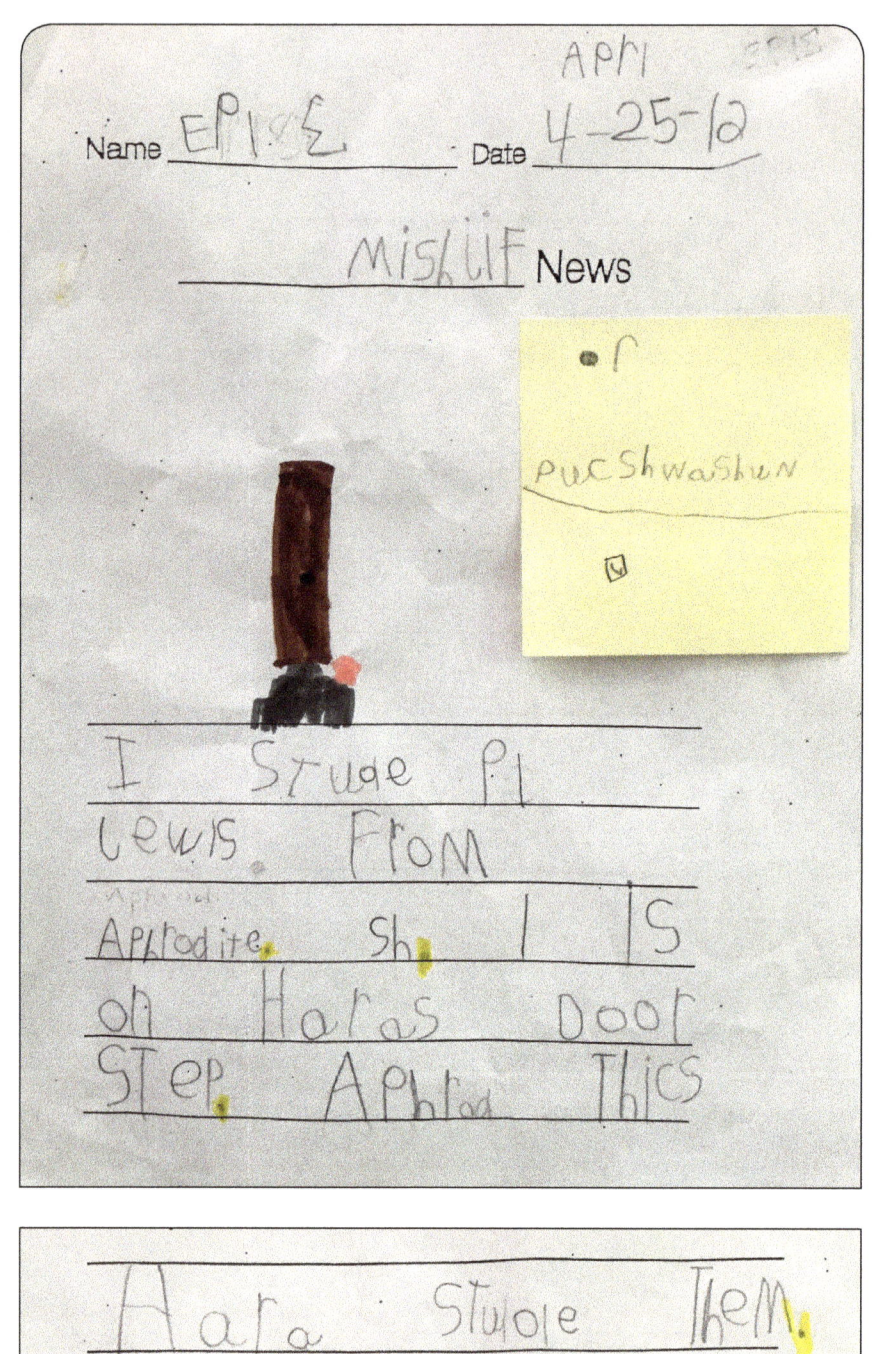

Instead of Weekend News, we wrote *Greek*end News one Monday morning, getting into our newly assigned "Golden Apple" characters. Bella, embracing her naughty side as the goddess of discord, wrote "Mischief News:" *I stole 19 jewels from Aphrodite. Shhh. 1 is on Hera's doorstep. Aphrodite thinks Hera stole them.* The sticky note reminds her of her self-selected goal to use punctuation.

Not all children were able to make the mental leap to take on a character they'd only just met, so we read accounts of Hermes's soccer game and Pelius's fun at Katie's birthday party. Ada wasn't sure how to write as the narrator, so she borrowed Olive's character, Aphrodite. Cate attempted to translate her news into Greek, using her new knowledge of the Greek alphabet!

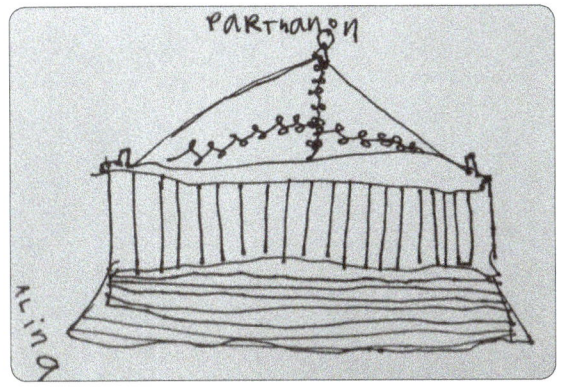 

Alina's drawing of the Parthenon shows a beginning understanding of perspective: notice the way she has drawn the steps broader at the bottom as they would really appear, giving herself diagonal guidelines to show the slope. At right, a coil pot inspired by Greek amphorae. Some students are able to achieve a narrower neck and flared rim; for others the challenge of neatly stacking the coils is enough.

Mount Olympus, populated by clothespin gods and goddesses

Some scenes from "The Golden Apple":

CONNECTED CONTENT

Cambium Vol. 4, No. 3: "Don't Throw Thunderbolts: Thematic Planning & Teaching in the K-1 Classroom"

Cambium Vol. 2, No. 3: "What Could Be Wong With Such Wuv? Formal and Informal Role-Playing"

These articles are appended at the end of this unit. To read them in their original contexts, please download the issues "Big Ideas for Curious Minds" and "Arts As Core Content" at arborcenterforteaching.org/cambium.

BIBLIOGRAPHY

Picture Books & Read-Alouds:

Aliki. *The gods and goddesses of Olympus.* New York, NY: Hyperion, 1994.

Amery, Heather, illus. by Linda Edwards. *Greek myths for young children.* London: Usborne, 2000.

D'Aulaire, Ingri & Edgar Parin. *D'Aulaire's book of Greek myths.* Garden City, NY: Doubleday, 1962.

Hutton, Warwick. *The Trojan horse.* New York, NY: Macmillan, 1992.

Little, Emily, illus. by Michael Eagle. *The Trojan horse: how the Greeks won the war* (Step into Reading series). New York, NY: Random House, 1998.

Lock, Deborah. *Greek myths* (DK Readers Level 3). New York, NY: DK Publishing, 2008.

Mayer, Marianna, illus. by Kinuko Y. Craft. *Pegasus.* New York, NY: William Morrow & Co, 1998.

Osborne, Mary Pope. *Tales from the Odyssey* (series). New York, NY: Hyperion, 2003, 2004.

O'Malley, Kevin. *Mount Olympus basketball.* New York, NY: Walker & Co, 1993.

Philip, Neil, illus. by Peter Malone. *The adventures of Odysseus.* London: Orion Children's Books, 1996.

Rylant, Cynthia. *The beautiful stories of life: six Greek myths, retold.* New York, NY: HMH Books for Young Readers, 2009.

Turnbull, Ann, illus. by Sarah Young. *Greek myths.* Somerville, MA: Candlewick, 2010.

Williams, Marcia. *Greek myths.* Somerville, MA: Candlewick, 2011.

Williams, Marcia. *The Iliad and the Odyssey.* London: Walker Books, Ltd., 2006.

Nonfiction:

Chattington, Jenny. *The ancient Greeks activity book*. London: The British Museum Press, 1986.

Curlee, Lynn. *Parthenon*. New York, NY: Atheneum, 2004.

Deschamps-Lequime, Sophie and Denise Vernerey. *The ancient Greeks: in the land of the gods* (Peoples of the Past series). Brookfield, CT: Millbrook Press, 1992.

Greig, Clarence. *Greece: great civilization*. London: Ladybird Books, 1974.

Jones, John Ellis. *Ancient Greece*. London: Kingfisher Books, 1983.

Loverance, Rowena. *Ancient Greece* (See Through History series). New York, NY: Viking/Penguin, 1992.

MacDonald, Fiona. *A Greek temple*. New York, NY: Peter Bedrick Books, 1992.

MacDonald, Fiona. *Greeks built temples, and other questions about ancient Greece*. New York, NY: Kingfisher, 1997.

Martell, Mary Hazel. *Myths and civilization of the ancient Greeks*. New York, NY: Peter Bedrick Books, 1998.

Pearson, Anne. *Ancient Greece* (DK Eyewitness series). New York, NY: DK Publishing, 2007.

Pearson, Anne. *What do we know about the Greeks*. New York, NY: Peter Bedrick Books, 1992.

Cambium

INNOVATIVE K-8 CURRICULUM FROM THE ARBOR SCHOOL OF ARTS & SCIENCES

DON'T THROW THUNDERBOLTS
THEMATIC PLANNING & TEACHING IN THE K-1 CLASSROOM

by Felicity Nunley, grade K-1

It's early May in the Primary Nest and the children are at work in the classroom. During this morning Choice time, some children are in the dress-up area donning togas and drinking from a golden goblet, re-enacting the story of the Golden Apple. Several children are practicing writing their own names and their parents' and their pets' names in Greek. One child is writing a book about mythological Greek creatures, carefully drawing nine heads on a hydra. At tabletops, some children are building temples, using blocks from the block area, erecting cylinders and rectangular prisms on a large sheet of graph paper, carefully balancing a triangular pediment on a row of columns.

During this part of the day, the line between work and play is especially blurry. But looking at the same scene again, we see children reading, writing, researching, retelling a story, and gaining familiarity with geometric solids. And almost without exception, the children are absorbed in their work—work that is entirely elective and a productive extension of work they began during more structured class times.

Making the hard work of learning to read and write compelling, something one yearns to do during one's free time, is the magic of teaching thematically. The theme of the classroom provides a rich and compelling context in which to build the burgeoning skills of young readers and writers. Imagine the thrill of the five-year-old who, guided by the strong clue of the initial letter, recognizes the word "Zeus," or the beginning writer who finds himself able to hand-letter a sign for the dress-up area to remind the gods and goddesses, "Don't throw thunderbolts." Indeed, the theme is the soil that nourishes the habits of mind we hope our young students will develop.

Some people are surprised to learn that we study Ancient Greece in the kindergarten and first-grade classes at Arbor. In fact, our study of the Greeks is one of the richest themes we undertake. The tales of the imperfect gods and goddesses, jealous, greedy, and selfish as they often can be, are endlessly compelling to young students who are themselves learning to share and work in close concert with others. Sharing such stories is central to building our classroom community and our collective knowledge, both social and academic. As natural collectors of facts and statistics, K-1 students savor the details of each god's exploits and affiliations; they love to craft cards or booklets of the complete set of the twelve Olympian heroes. And needless to say, the material provides rich fodder for integrating reading, writing, and math.

So how to start? The yearlong themes that frame the K-8 curriculum at Arbor are broad and general, but rich with possibility and content. In one of the two rotating Primary class themes, the children study Journeys, exploring territory real and imagined, near and far. Just as the child is reaching a developmental point at which she is ready to make the stretch from home to school, it is appropriate to introduce her to the "home-adventure-home" cycle in literature, science, and history. Our year begins on the water as we consider the properties that allow a vessel to float and immerse ourselves in the story of the Mayflower, of a handful of families making a great ocean crossing to find a new home. We study the migrations of whales, the most remarkable sea-voyagers of all. Finally, we turn to the venturesome Greek heroes of old: no greater example of "home-adventure-home" exists than the *Odyssey*.

Whether we are studying the Greeks, boats, or the human body, the process of designing a thematic unit is the same. It is an exercise in editing—deciding what is essential and captivating content and what is of particular use to further our curricular aims. During the process it is important to keep asking critical questions: *Is it authentic? What is the real work that is being accomplished?*

1. Identify central curricular concepts

Remembering that the theme really serves the larger purposes of the curricular goals, my teaching partner and I broadly outline what we would like to accomplish in a year with this batch of students. In the kindergarten and first-grade classroom, our large academic purposes are that students learn that reading and writing have real purposes; that they experience that the world can be quantified and develop tools and strategies for mathematical expression; that they start to recognize and anticipate patterns, understanding that the world has order; and that they maintain and feed their sense of wonder about the world.

To study Journeys throughout the year provides opportunity to serve all these aims. Noticing and mapping landmarks on the ride from home to school encourages looking out the window of the car and getting to know one's own particular landscape. Keeping a journal in the voice of an actual passenger on the Mayflower provides motivation to practice new writing skills. Learning about the feats of migrating animals inspires wonder in us all. Reveling in ancient tales of skullduggery and derring-do, in the bravery, wit, and persistence of characters in the oldest stories, nourishes children's imagination and developing sense of ethics.

Traditionally, we have studied the ancient Greeks during the spring semester. At this point in the year, many of our students can practice reading with expression, summarizing stories, and articulating the main message of a story. Other readers are starting to recognize words and continue to use picture clues and context to make meaning from a text. At this point, we have practiced letter formation and are ready for longer pieces of handwriting practice, paying particular attention to end punctuation and conventions of capitalization. Mathematically, the Primaries are ready to explore and codify the properties of shapes and geometric solids. Also, we are ready for an introduction to multiplication and division, as well as continuing to write and solve our own word problems.

2. Educate myself

When turning my attention to the thematic content, I allow myself a good amount of time to stew. Our topics are genuinely rich for learners of any age, and the children can sense their teachers' authentic interest. I read adult and children's books about our themes and try to immerse myself in the topic. When planning the Journeys year, I am sure to take a few myself, documenting the steps of my journey to share with my students in the fall. What better excuse to spend some time messing about in boats than preparing to teach about boats? In the spring, I reread the Greek myths, eat Greek food, sift through artifacts from a long-ago trip to Greece, and look up the current temperature in Athens.

3. Draft

As I stew, I jot down notes, thinking of possibilities, but commit to nothing. Often this takes the form of a web or a hasty list. After a while, I look back at my jottings and evaluate what seems essential, what might be especially attractive to this particular group of children, and what might lend itself well to our curricular priorities. As I look over my notes, I ask myself, "Is there a balance of academic, pencil-and-paper work with the make-and-do? What are the big questions the topic provokes? Are there opportunities for authentic experiences to make topics as remote and distant as Ancient Greece authentic and tangible? Is there an appropriate balance of active, physical work with quiet, reflective work?" At this point, it is appropriate to consider what is essential because it's tradition, still cherished by children who have moved on to the upper grades or beyond, and what we might jettison from previous years.

4. Start at the End

At this point, plans that seem amorphous and unwieldy must be wrestled into some sort of timeline. Typically, our units culminate in a community celebration, a fixed date on the calendar. We invite parents and the children's older buddies into the classroom to admire our hard work, to read through books we have written, and to try their hand at some of the experiences we have enjoyed. Bringing the unit to fruition on this precise date and time can feel a bit like airlifting an elephant on to an olive. So we start at the end and identify a thematic focus for each week. Under that umbrella, we identify the week's reading, writing, and math foci. A week devoted to Athena might inspire writing about her in our gods and goddesses book, trying our hands at weaving and working with clay, looking at the Parthenon, and identifying the geometry in Greek temples.

Greek temples drawn by Emil and Siddha

Again, we return to our curricular priorities and identify our next best move. Each year, our priorities shift in response to the make-up of the class. Is this a group that could rise to the challenge of reading chapters of the *Odyssey*? Does a young class need more time building temples?

So what might this all look like? Each year, it looks a little different, with the class developing interests of its own. Our weekly class newsletter is effective in capturing snapshots of the week's work:

> "Before delving into the Greek creation myth, we asked the class to imagine what there was before there was anything. Some children imagined utter darkness, others imagined dusty plains and craters, and others imagined endless mountains. Many of us knew about the Big Bang. We read several creation myths from a variety of traditions that explained how the world came to be, including a tale from Siberia in which the world's creator sprang from a pea

pod…. On Thursday, we wrote a creation myth of our own: a rollicking tale that includes a moose, a frog, and some ants. We illustrated the tale with large tempera paintings that hang on a mural in the classroom."

"We had some fun telling math stories about Zeus and Hera: 'At the banquet, there were six pomegranates. Zeus ate four. How many were left?' 'Hera's peacock had 10 feathers. Zeus plucked five for a pillow. How many were left?' We wrote our own math problems, being sure to end with the question, 'How many were left?' On Friday we solved each other's problems."

"Inspired by Apollo, we made a class set of lyres with boxes and rubber bands. We hypothesized about what makes a string make a high sound or a low sound. Is it the thickness of the rubber band? The length of the rubber band? The tightness or looseness of the rubber band? Does the shape of the box matter? Does the material the box is made from matter? With partners, the kids set about the task of making a lyre that made low tones, medium tones, and high tones. As they worked, we listened for supportive and productive communication when they encountered unanticipated design challenges and found that their initial assumptions were not always correct."

As I write this, our class has become captivated by the story of Theseus in King Minos's Labyrinth. Students are building mazes with geoboards and designing mazes on paper. Several children are planning "Maze Day," signing classmates up for a maze elective. We've never done it before, but such opportunities to improvise and let students take the lead are often among the richest veins in thematic teaching. Stay tuned!

Siddha, a first-grader, independently sewed her own Greek robe by hand. At right, a page from Jesse's book of Greek gods and goddesses.

Cambium

INNOVATIVE K-8 CURRICULUM FROM THE ARBOR SCHOOL OF ARTS & SCIENCES

WHAT COULD BE WONG WITH SUCH WUV?
FORMAL AND INFORMAL ROLE-PLAYING IN THE PRIMARY CLASSROOM

by Felicity Nunley and Lori Pressman

"I see J1! I see J1!"

It is early morning in the Primary classroom and Abe and Maddie are in the whale research lab that has been set up in the block area. Cardboard tubes are taped to cereal boxes to serve as telescopes. The children type at computers made from shoeboxes and a discarded keyboard. On the cardboard monitor, they have drawn a picture of an orca; with a few quick maneuvers of the wine cork mouse, they identify it as J1, the patriarch of a resident pod of orcas in the San Juan Islands that we read about yesterday. At work in the lab, Maddie's and Abe's excitement is as palpable as any "real" whale watcher's.

Throughout their days at Arbor, students have many opportunities to try on roles both formally and informally. Role-playing is natural and spontaneous to the five- and six-year-old child. At recess, elaborate narratives are spun as they become mama kitties and lost orphan kitties. When this energy is invited into the classroom, Primaries readily become whale researchers during Choice time, integrating the information they have learned in class. We hear them in the whale lab discussing the whale they have sighted: "I think it's a humpback! No, wait, it can't be a humpback. It has teeth!"

A child's natural inclination to play and assume roles is a powerful device for enlivening curriculum, making content meaningful in personal and authentic ways. By stepping into a role as someone else, students can imagine how things might have been long ago and far away. Primaries learn to identify with characters in history when they are assigned roles of actual passengers as they study the Mayflower. Nor do they abandon role-playing after the Primary years: as Juniors they become members of the Corps of Discovery, experiencing the impulse of an explorer, eager to see what is around the next corner as they battle the blackberries in the woods to chart a remote corner of the campus. They travel the Oregon Trail as pioneers, budgeting for the purchase and weight of supplies and reenacting the fording of rivers and the scaling of passes

> We set up inquiry stations for each new unit by brainstorming with the children what tools we might need to become whale researchers, entomologists, passengers on the Mayflower, or whatever our studies require. The Primaries are quick to leap into construction mode in our "junk box" building area, and the subsequent play at the inquiry station is self-sustaining.

with red wagon prairie schooners. As Intermediate fourth and fifth graders, they will become denizens of a 12th-century European city to explore the effects of power and privilege (or the lack thereof) on daily medieval life.

Every two years in the Primary classrooms at Arbor, role-playing is formalized at a new level as we prepare a theatrical production of a retelling of The Judgment of Paris, a dramatic tale of jealousy and problem-solving set among the Greek gods and goddesses of Mt. Olympus. We begin by preparing the students with an introduction to the Greek pantheon. As a class, we read the stories of the Greek myths and learn the biographies of the players, each child compiling a book of 12 gods and goddesses with a few simple facts and illustrations. Naturally, the kids begin taking on these roles during recess and Choice times as they pull out togas and thunderbolts from the dress-up box. Enterprising runners tape feathers to their sneakers in the style of Hermes. Athena straps a stuffed animal owl to her shoulder.

D'Aulaires' Book of Greek Myths, by Ingri D'Aulaire and Edgar Parin D'Aulaire, is a favorite resource.

Two years ago we were fortunate to have a teaching apprentice with a background in the classics and a desire to lead our students deeper into those ancient, enthralling tales. Jenny Lowe Cook remembers her transformation into Homer the bard:

Here is what some would call a gamble: teaching ancient Greek epic to modern day kindergarteners and first graders. Homer's Odyssey is so ancient, so thoroughly foreign; with its warriors, monsters, deities, and very hard-to-pronounce names, what is the use of telling it to such young children? Won't they be confused and bored by it all?

I had grown up hearing stories of the Greek gods and goddesses and the retelling of the Trojan war from both the Greek and Trojan perspectives. I had read Homer and Vergil and loved those epic stories dearly. Ever since I had heard that Arbor Primaries devoted a part of their year to studying the Greeks, I was excited to teach that part of the curriculum. But the Fates, it seems, had different plans. I ended up teaching oceanography to the Intermediates while the Primaries were studying the Greeks and getting ready to perform their play about the legend of the golden apple. I wanted to stay involved and share my knowledge of ancient Greek mythology, but could only find one hour a week in my schedule that would work. Laura Frizzell graciously gave me that hour of her music time with the Primaries to tell stories instead.

I decided to tell them the story of the Odyssey, all about Odysseus's wanderings and misadventures in trying to get back to his native Greek homeland after the fall of Troy. I used an excellent picture book retelling by Geraldine McCaughrean and Victor Ambrus as my guide to remind me of the many stops that Odysseus made along the way.

The Odyssey, retold by Geraldine McCaughrean and illustrated by Victor G. Ambrus, is now out of print, but many of McCaughrean's tellings of the Greek myths and legends should be available in your library.

I'm not sure when in the process inspiration struck me to dress up as Homer and to tell the story as a bard. I knew that I had to keep the 36 Primaries engaged and interested for about an hour of storytelling, and as I discovered, a few props go a long way. I assembled a small bag of shawls and fabric scraps, found a zither-like instrument in the storage attic, and fashioned a chiton of sorts from an old red bedsheet. I wrote myself a Post-it note of highlights to aid my memory and kept it in the palm of my hand, just in case the Muse of good memory left me stranded! I remember sitting there on a little stool shivering in a red bedsheet and strumming an outrageously out-of-tune toy zither while the Primaries filed in slowly and sat wonderingly before me in the Arena. I was no longer Jenny the apprentice; I was Homer the bard.

I wasn't sure how they would react to my costume; in fact, I wasn't sure how they would react to any of it! Even with my props and my pretense, would they just lose interest? In those few moments of waiting for everyone to settle down, I experienced a wave of stage fright. I had found these stories fascinating as a child, but maybe that was just because my father is a classicist! What if these stories were going to go over their heads? But looking at their eager and expectant faces, I realized that once upon a time, there were little children who had sat at Homer's feet listening to his stories, too. I launched into my invocation of the Muse, and she must have heard my cry. The children sat spellbound and listened to the first part of the story for the rest of the hour. I occasionally chose some of them to be actors and participants in my story, perhaps giving them a prop or draping them in a shawl so that they could get into their role. Sometimes I whispered in their ear the "lines" they were supposed to say; other times I just stood behind them and said it for them, and guided them around the "stage". I marveled at their cooperation and eagerness to be part of the story, even though they quickly saw that it was not their chance to reinvent the story. They were content and excited to become living props, and sometimes I would hear them bragging to each other as they returned to their classroom, "I was Odysseus today!"

I often began by asking for someone to sum up what had happened in the prior week's storytelling session, and I was amazed how many hands flew up into the air. Their recollection of the details of the story was impressive. That's because visual storytelling is so powerful, and especially when the children are given the chance to be inserted into the story, for however brief a moment. The story unfolded episodically over eight Fridays and by the last one I was sorry to bring the story to an end. But the beautiful thing about working with children is that their imaginations never come to an end; even when one story is finished, they are always ready to begin with a new one of their own.

> Studying the myths and literature of the ancient Greeks offers a chance to help young children grapple with some of the most powerful themes in human life. What does it mean to be a hero? What are the consequences of acting in greed, rage, or jealousy? How can we stay faithful to the people we love?

For many of our students, Jenny's gentle maneuvering and whispered prompts constituted their first experience as actors. But young children, including pre-readers, memorize lines quite facilely; some of our Primaries have been known to memorize the entire play during home practice with their parents. The script for "The Golden Apple" was written by two Primary students ten years ago and has enjoyed several stagings over the years. Each year the script is altered a bit to accommodate the make-up of the class. A comic role for Dionysus was written in one year and replaced by a musical Apollo the next. At this point, the tradition of the Greek play carries its own momentum. The whole school anticipates the production and is nostalgic for those days as Helen of Troy or Aphrodite. Ask any Arbor Senior who he was in the play; he will not hesitate in his reply and might even offer a line or two.

When we are ready to launch our more formal production of "The Golden Apple," the first job is casting. The assignment of roles has been done in a variety of ways, from drawing sticks from a bag for chance assignments to careful, intentional teacher decisions. In either case, there is an opportunity for students to stretch themselves. A student may have a chance to get to know a character he already identifies with in greater depth. After playing Hestia for weeks in the dress-up corner, Peach got to perform an idealized Hestia on stage, batting her eyes as she swept the hearth in domestic bliss. The casting can also be an opportunity for a student to try on a persona that is distinctly other than her own. Purposefully, we have assigned the role of angry, jealous Eris to shy and retiring students, challenging them to develop a strong voice. As they embody the goddess of discord, the students learn to assert themselves in uncharacteristic rage. Similarly, the play offers a new situation in which students can challenge themselves and find success. In class, a child might be a struggling and reluctant reader. Cast as a narrator of the play, he can rise to the challenge of reading and learning many lines. In some cases, the voice discovered on the stage will never recede into quiet again. Bea's belting out her lines has officially made obsolete the impression that she could only be a shy and quiet girl.

Max, Norris, and Holden as Greek gods

Through the play, the children get to experience that many hands really do make light work and that everyone's contributions are important. Everyone has a job, the completion of which is critical to the success of the play before a real audience. Lines and cues must be learned, props need to be constructed, backdrops painted, programs written. The art of being backstage, quietly waiting one's turn to perform, is not the least of the skills the Primaries work to hone.

Even the parents get in on the excitement of the play. Indeed, a mother who is a theater professional first showed us it was possible to direct five- to seven-year-olds in a production of this scale. In the weeks before the performance, parents share their toga-making expertise, consult each other about Greek sandal-tying techniques and laurel crown-weaving tips, and help children rehearse their scenes. We also invite parents to help make spanakopita and baklava for a reception after the play.

On the day of the performance, there is a palpable sense of excitement in the hushed amphitheater as the actors take their places. Some musicians are playing Greek incidental music; the columns with their pizza-box Doric capitals are standing almost straight. The audience is rapt as the wiggly-toothed actors deliver their lines. Finally, we get to the ominous conclusion of the play—the forbidden love of Helen and Paris. With great emotion, our Hermes asks, "What could be wong with such wuv?"

The script for "The Golden Apple" is available for download at arborcenterforteaching.org/s/GoldenApple.pdf.

APPENDIX: COMMON CORE, NEXT GENERATION SCIENCE, AND NATIONAL GEOGRAPHY STANDARDS ALIGNMENT ANALYSIS

Leaves, Arbor students of 1995-96

UNIT 1: LITERACY

The Mouse Boats and Buoyancy curriculum aligns with these Common Core ELA aims:

Writing: Text Types and Purposes	*CCSS.ELA-LITERACY.W.K.3/1.3* Use a combination of drawing, dictating, and writing to write narratives in which they recount two or more appropriately sequenced events, include some details regarding what happened, may use temporal words to signal event order, and provide some sense of closure.
Speaking and Listening: Comprehension and Collaboration	*CCSS.ELA-LITERACY.SL.K.1/1.1* Participate in collaborative conversations with peers and adults in small and larger groups. *CCSS.ELA-LITERACY.SL.K.2/1.2* Ask and answer questions about key details in a text read aloud or information presented orally or through other media. *CCSS.ELA-LITERACY.SL.K.3/1.3* Ask and answer questions about what a speaker says in order to gather additional information or clarify something that is not understood.
Presentation of Knowledge and Ideas	*CCSS.ELA-LITERACY.SL.K.4/1.4* Describe familiar people, places, things, and events and, with prompting and support, provide additional detail. *CCSS.ELA-LITERACY.SL.K.5/1.5* Add drawings or other visual displays to descriptions when appropriate to clarify ideas, thoughts, and feelings. *CCSS.ELA-LITERACY.W.4.2.B/5.2.B* Speak audibly and express thoughts, feelings, and ideas clearly.

JOURNEYS

UNIT 1: MATHEMATICS

The Mouse Boats and Buoyancy curriculum aligns with these Common Core Standards for Math Practice:

Math Practice

CCSS.MATH.PRACTICE.MP2
Reason abstractly and quantitatively.

CCSS.MATH.PRACTICE.MP3
Construct viable arguments and critique the reasoning of others.

CCSS.MATH.PRACTICE.MP5
Use appropriate tools strategically.

... and with these Common Core Standards for Math Content:

Counting and Cardinality

CCSS.MATH.CONTENT.K.CC.B.4
Understand the relationship between numbers and quantities; connect counting to cardinality.

CCSS.MATH.CONTENT.K.CC.B.5
Count to answer "how many?" questions about as many as 20 things.

CCSS.MATH.CONTENT.K.CC.C.6
Identify whether the number of objects in one group is greater than, less than, or equal to the number of objects in another group, e.g., by using matching and counting strategies.

Measurement and Data

CCSS.MATH.CONTENT.K.MD.A.1
Describe measurable attributes of objects, such as length or weight. Describe several measurable attributes of a single object.

CCSS.MATH.CONTENT.K.MD.A.2
Directly compare two objects with a measurable attribute in common, to see which object has "more of"/"less of" the attribute, and describe the difference.

CCSS.MATH.CONTENT.K.MD.B.3
Classify objects into given categories; count the numbers of objects in each category and sort the categories by count.

UNIT 1: SCIENCE

The Mouse Boats and Buoyancy curriculum aligns with these Next Generation Science Standards:

Science and Engineering Practices	*Practice 1: Asking questions*
	Practice 2: Developing and using models
	Practice 3: Planning and carrying out investigations
	Practice 4: Analyzing and interpreting data
	Practice 5: Using mathematics and computational thinking
	Practice 6: Constructing explanations
	Practice 7: Engaging in argument from evidence
	Practice 8: Obtaining, evaluating, and communicating information
Disciplinary Core Ideas in Forces and Interactions	*PS2.A: Forces and Motion*
	PS2.B: Types of Interactions
Disciplinary Core Ideas in Engineering Design	*ETS1.A: Defining and Delimiting Engineering Problems*
	ETS1.B: Developing Possible Solutions
	ETS1.C: Optimizing the Design Solution
Crosscutting Concepts	*Cause and Effect* Simple tests can be designed to gather evidence to support or refute student ideas about causes. *Structure and Function* The shape and stability of structures of natural and designed objects are related to their function(s).

UNIT 2: LITERACY

The Mapmaking curriculum aligns with these Common Core ELA aims:

Foundational Skills: Print Concepts

CCSS.ELA-LITERACY.RF.K.1a
Follow words from left to right, top to bottom, and page by page.

CCSS.ELA-LITERACY.RF.K.1b
Recognize that spoken words are represented in written language by specific sequences of letters.

CCSS.ELA-LITERACY.RF.K.1c
Understand that words are separated by spaces in print.

Language: Conventions of Standard English

CCSS.ELA-LITERACY.L.K.1a/1.1a
Print many (Kindergartners) or all (First Graders) upper- and lowercase letters.

CCSS.ELA-LITERACY.L.K.1f
Produce and expand complete sentences in shared language activities.

CCSS.ELA-LITERACY.L.1.2d
Use conventional spelling for words with common spelling patterns and for frequently occurring irregular words.

CCSS.ELA-LITERACY.L.1.2e
Spell untaught words phonetically, drawing on phonemic awareness and spelling conventions.

Language: Vocabulary Acquisition and Use

CCSS.ELA-LITERACY.L.1.5c
Identify real-life connections between words and their use.

CCSS.ELA-LITERACY.L.1.6
Use words and phrases acquired through conversations, reading and being read to, and responding to texts.

UNIT 2: MATHEMATICS

The Mapmaking curriculum aligns with these Common Core Standards for Math Practice:

Math Practice	*CCSS.MATH.PRACTICE.MP2* Reason abstractly and quantitatively.
	CCSS.MATH.PRACTICE.MP5 Use appropriate tools strategically.
	CCSS.MATH.PRACTICE.MP6 Attend to precision.
	CCSS.MATH.PRACTICE.MP7 Look for and make use of structure.

... and with these Common Core Standards for Math Content:

Counting and Cardinality	*CCSS.MATH.CONTENT.K.CC.A.3* Write numbers from 0 to 20.
Numbers and Operations in Base Ten	*CCSS.MATH.CONTENT.1.NBT.A.1* Count to 120, starting at any number less than 120. In this range, read and write numerals and represent a number of objects with a written numeral.
Measurement and Data	*CCSS.MATH.CONTENT.K.MD.A.1* Describe measurable attributes of objects, such as length.
	CCSS.MATH.CONTENT.1.MD.A.2 Express the length of an object as a whole number of length units.
Geometry	*CCSS.MATH.CONTENT.K.G.A.3* Identify shapes as two-dimensional or three-dimensional.
	CCSS.MATH.CONTENT.5.G.A.1 Use a pair of perpendicular number lines, to define a coordinate system, with the intersection of the lines.

JOURNEYS

UNIT 2: SCIENCE

The Mapmaking curriculum aligns with these Next Generation Science Standards:

Science and Engineering Practices	*Practice 2: Developing and using models*
	Practice 4: Analyzing and interpreting data
	Practice 8: Obtaining, evaluating, and communicating information
Disciplinary Core Ideas in Interdependent Relationships in Ecosystems	*LS1.C: Organization for Matter and Energy Flow in Organisms*
	LS4.D: Biodiversity and Humans
	ESS3.C: Human Impacts on Earth Systems
Disciplinary Core Ideas in Earth's Systems	*ESS2.C: The Roles of Water in Earth's Surface Processes*
Crosscutting Concepts	*Cause and Effect* Events have causes that generate observable patterns. *Structure and Function* The shape and stability of structures of natural and designed objects are related to their function(s).

UNIT 2: GEOGRAPHY

The Mapmaking curriculum aligns with these National Geography Standards:

The World in Spatial Terms	1. How to use maps and other geographic representations, tools, and technologies to acquire, process, and report information.
	2. How to use mental maps to organize information about people, places, and environments.
	3. How to analyze the spatial organization of people, places, and environments on Earth's surface.
Places and Regions	4. The physical and human characteristics of places.
Physical Systems	7. The physical processes that shape the patterns of Earth's surface.
	8. The characteristics and spatial distribution of ecosystems on Earth's surface.
Human Systems	9. The characteristics, distribution, and migration of human populations on Earth's surface.
	12. The process, patterns, and functions of human settlement.
Environment and Society	14. How human actions modify the physical environment.
	15. How physical systems affect human systems.
The Uses of Geography	18. To apply geography to interpret the present and plan for the future.

UNIT 3: LITERACY

The Imaginary Journeys curriculum aligns with these Common Core ELA aims:

Reading Informational Text: Key Ideas and Details	*CCSS.ELA-LITERACY.RL.K.1/1.1* Ask and answer questions about key details in a text. *CCSS.ELA-LITERACY.RL.K.2/1.2* Retell stories, including key details, and demonstrate understanding of their central message or lesson. *CCSS.ELA-LITERACY.RL.K.3/1.3* Describe characters, settings, and major events in a story, using key details.
Reading Literature: Integration of Knowledge and Ideas	*CCSS.ELA-LITERACY.RL.1.7* Use illustrations and details in a story to describe its characters, setting, or events. *CCSS.ELA-LITERACY.RL.K.9/1.9* Compare and contrast the adventures and experiences of characters in stories.
Range of Reading and Level of Text Complexity	*CCSS.ELA-LITERACY.RL.K.10* Actively engage in group reading activities with purpose and understanding.
Foundational Skills: Print Concepts	*CCSS.ELA-LITERACY.RF.K.1a* Follow words from left to right, top to bottom, and page by page. *CCSS.ELA-LITERACY.RF.K.1b* Recognize that spoken words are represented in written language by specific sequences of letters. *CCSS.ELA-LITERACY.RF.K.1c* Understand that words are separated by spaces in print.

Writing: Text Types and Purposes	*CCSS.ELA-LITERACY.W.K.3/1.3* Use a combination of drawing, dictating, and writing to write narratives in which they recount two or more appropriately sequenced events, include some details regarding what happened, may use temporal words to signal event order, and provide some sense of closure.
Language: Conventions of Standard English	*CCSS.ELA-LITERACY.L.K.1a/1.1a* Print many (Kindergartners) or all (First Graders) upper- and lowercase letters. *CCSS.ELA-LITERACY.L.K.1f* Produce and expand complete sentences in shared language activities. *CCSS.ELA-LITERACY.L.1.2d* Use conventional spelling for words with common spelling patterns and for frequently occurring irregular words. *CCSS.ELA-LITERACY.L.1.2e* Spell untaught words phonetically, drawing on phonemic awareness and spelling conventions.
Vocabulary Acquisition and Use	*CCSS.ELA-LITERACY.L.K.6/1.6* Use words and phrases acquired through conversations, reading and being read to, and responding to texts.

UNIT 3: MATHEMATICS

The Imaginary Journeys curriculum aligns with these Common Core Standards for Math Practice:

Math Practice

CCSS.MATH.PRACTICE.MP2
Reason abstractly and quantitatively.

CCSS.MATH.PRACTICE.MP4
Model with mathematics.

CCSS.MATH.PRACTICE.MP5
Use appropriate tools strategically.

CCSS.MATH.PRACTICE.MP8
Look for and express regularity in repeated reasoning.

... and with these Common Core Standards for Math Content:

Operations and Algebraic Thinking

CCSS.MATH.CONTENT.K.OA.A.2
Solve addition and subtraction word problems by using objects or drawings to represent the problem.

CCSS.MATH.CONTENT.K.OA.A.4
For any number from 1 to 9, find the number that makes 10 when added to the given number, e.g., by using objects or drawings, and record the answer with a drawing or equation.

CCSS.MATH.CONTENT.2.OA.C.3
Determine whether a group of objects has an odd or even number of members, e.g., by pairing objects or counting them by 2s.

CCSS.MATH.CONTENT.2.OA.C.4
Use addition to find the total number of objects arranged in rectangular arrays.

CCSS.MATH.CONTENT.3.OA.D.9
Identify arithmetic patterns.

Numbers and Operations in Base Ten	*CCSS.MATH.CONTENT.1.NBT.A.1* Count to 120, starting at any number less than 120. In this range, read and write numerals and represent a number of objects with a written numeral.
Geometry	*CCSS.MATH.CONTENT.K.G.A.3* Identify shapes as two-dimensional or three-dimensional. *CCSS.MATH.CONTENT.5.G.A.1* Use a pair of perpendicular number lines, to define a coordinate system, with the intersection of the lines.

UNIT 3: SCIENCE

The Imaginary Journeys curriculum aligns with these Next Generation Science Standards:

Science and Engineering Practices	*Practice 2: Developing and using models* *Practice 5: Using mathematics and computational thinking* *Practice 8: Obtaining, evaluating, and communicating information*
Crosscutting Concepts	*Patterns* Patterns in the natural and human designed world can be observed and used as evidence. *Systems and System Models* Systems in the natural and designed world have parts that work together.

JOURNEYS

UNIT 3: GEOGRAPHY

The Imaginary Journeys curriculum aligns with these National Geography Standards:

The World in Spatial Terms	1. How to use maps and other geographic representations, tools, and technologies to acquire, process, and report information.
	2. How to use mental maps to organize information about people, places, and environments.
	3. How to analyze the spatial organization of people, places, and environments on Earth's surface.
Places and Regions	4. The physical and human characteristics of places.
Physical Systems	8. The characteristics and spatial distribution of ecosystems on Earth's surface.
Human Systems	9. The characteristics, distribution, and migration of human populations on Earth's surface.
Environment and Society	15. How physical systems affect human systems.

UNIT 4: LITERACY

The *Mayflower* Journey curriculum aligns with these Common Core ELA aims:

Reading Informational Text: Key Ideas and Details	*CCSS.ELA-LITERACY.RL.K.1/1.1* Ask and answer questions about key details in a text. *CCSS.ELA-LITERACY.RL.K.2/1.2* Identify the main topic and retell key details of a text. *CCSS.ELA-LITERACY.RL.K.3/1.3* Describe the connection between two individuals, events, ideas, or pieces of information in a text.
Reading Information: Craft and Structure	*CCSS.ELA-LITERACY.RI.K.4/1.4* Ask and answer questions to help determine or clarify the meaning of words and phrases in a text. *CCSS.ELA-LITERACY.RI.K.5* Identify the front cover, back cover, and title page of a book. *CCSS.ELA-LITERACY.RI.1.5* Know and use various text features to locate key facts or information in a text.
Reading Information: Integration of Knowledge and Ideas	*CCSS.ELA-LITERACY.RI.1.7* Use illustrations and details in a text to describe its key ideas.
Range of Reading and Level of Text Complexity	*CCSS.ELA-LITERACY.RL.K.10* Actively engage in group reading activities with purpose and understanding. *CCSS.ELA-LITERACY.RI.1.10* With prompting and support, read grade level informational texts.

Foundational Skills: Print Concepts	CCSS.ELA-LITERACY.RF.K.1c Understand that words are separated by spaces in print. CCSS.ELA-LITERACY.RF.1.1a Recognize the distinguishing features of a sentence (e.g., first word, capitalization, ending punctuation).
Writing: Text Types and Purposes	CCSS.ELA-LITERACY.W.K.3/1.3 Write narratives in which they recount two or more appropriately sequenced events, include some details regarding what happened, use temporal words to signal event order, and provide some sense of closure.
Production and Distribution of Writing	CCSS.ELA-LITERACY.W.K.5/1.5 With guidance and support from adults, focus on a topic, respond to questions and suggestions from peers, and add details to strengthen writing as needed.
Research to Build and Present Knowledge	CCSS.ELA-LITERACY.W.K.7/1.7 Participate in shared research and writing projects. CCSS.ELA-LITERACY.W.K.8/1.8 With guidance and support from adults, recall information from experiences or gather information from provided sources to answer a question.
Speaking and Listening: Comprehension and Collaboration	CCSS.ELA-LITERACY.SL.K.1/1.1 Participate in collaborative conversations with peers and adults in small and larger groups. CCSS.ELA-LITERACY.SL.K.2/1.2 Ask and answer questions about key details in a text read aloud or information presented orally or through other media. CCSS.ELA-LITERACY.SL.K.3/1.3 Ask and answer questions about what a speaker says in order to gather additional information or clarify something that is not understood.

Presentation of Knowledge and Ideas	*CCSS.ELA-LITERACY.SL.K.4/1.4* Describe people, places, things, and events with relevant details, expressing ideas and feelings clearly. *CCSS.ELA-LITERACY.SL.K.5/1.5* Add drawings or other visual displays to descriptions when appropriate to clarify ideas, thoughts, and feelings.
Language: Conventions of Standard English	*CCSS.ELA-LITERACY.L.K.1f* Produce and expand complete sentences in shared language activities. *CCSS.ELA-LITERACY.L.1.2d* Use conventional spelling for words with common spelling patterns and for frequently occurring irregular words. *CCSS.ELA-LITERACY.L.1.2e* Spell untaught words phonetically, drawing on phonemic awareness and spelling conventions.
Vocabulary Acquisition and Use	*CCSS.ELA-LITERACY.L.K.6/1.6* Use words and phrases acquired through conversations, reading and being read to, and responding to texts. *CCSS.ELA-LITERACY.W.K.5/1.5* With guidance and support from adults, focus on a topic, respond to questions and suggestions from peers, and add details to strengthen writing as needed.

UNIT 4: MATHEMATICS

The *Mayflower* Journey curriculum aligns with these Common Core Standards for Math Practice:

Math Practice

CCSS.MATH.PRACTICE.MP1
Make sense of problems and persevere in solving them.

CCSS.MATH.PRACTICE.MP2
Reason abstractly and quantitatively.

CCSS.MATH.PRACTICE.MP4
Model with mathematics.

CCSS.MATH.PRACTICE.MP5
Use appropriate tools strategically.

CCSS.MATH.PRACTICE.MP7
Look for and make use of structure.

... and with these Common Core Standards for Math Content:

Operations and Algebraic Thinking

CCSS.MATH.CONTENT.K.OA.A.1
Represent addition and subtraction with objects, fingers, mental images, drawings, sounds (e.g., claps), acting out situations, verbal explanations, expressions, or equations.

CCSS.MATH.CONTENT.K.OA.A.2
Solve addition and subtraction word problems, and add and subtract within 10, e.g., by using objects or drawings to represent the problem.

CCSS.MATH.CONTENT.1.OA.A.1
Use addition and subtraction within 20 to solve word problems by using objects, drawings, and equations.

CCSS.MATH.CONTENT.1.OA.B.3
Apply properties of operations as strategies to add and subtract.

Numbers and Operations in Base Ten	*CCSS.MATH.CONTENT.K.NBT.A.1* Compose and decompose numbers from 11 to 19 into ten and ones. *CCSS.MATH.CONTENT.1.NBT.B.2* Understand that the two digits of a two-digit number represent amounts of tens and ones. *CCSS.MATH.CONTENT.1.NBT.C.5* Given a two-digit number, mentally find 10 more or 10 less than the number, without having to count; explain the reasoning used.
Measurement and Data	*CCSS.MATH.CONTENT.K.MD.A.1* Describe measurable attributes of objects, such as length or weight. Describe several measurable attributes of a single object. *CCSS.MATH.CONTENT.K.MD.A.2* Directly compare two objects with a measurable attribute in common, to see which object has "more of"/"less of" the attribute, and describe the difference. *CCSS.MATH.CONTENT.K.MD.B.3* Classify objects into given categories; count the numbers of objects in each category and sort the categories by count. *CCSS.MATH.CONTENT.1.MD.A.2* Express the length of an object as a whole number of length units.
Geometry	*CCSS.MATH.CONTENT.K.G.A.3* Identify shapes as two-dimensional or three-dimensional.

UNIT 4: SCIENCE

The *Mayflower* Journey curriculum aligns with these Next Generation Science Standards:

Science and Engineering Practices	Practice 1: Asking questions
	Practice 2: Developing and using models
	Practice 5: Using mathematics and computational thinking
Disciplinary Core Ideas in Space Systems	ESS1.A: The Universe and its Stars
	ESS1.B: Earth and the Solar System
Crosscutting Concepts	Patterns Patterns in the natural world can be observed, used to describe phenomena, and used as evidence.

UNIT 4: GEOGRAPHY

The *Mayflower* Journey curriculum aligns with these National Geography Standards:

The World in Spatial Terms	1. How to use maps and other geographic representations, tools, and technologies to acquire, process, and report information.
	2. How to use mental maps to organize information about people, places, and environments.
	3. How to analyze the spatial organization of people, places, and environments on Earth's surface.
Human Systems	9. The characteristics, distribution, and migration of human populations on Earth's surface.
	11. The patterns and networks of economic interdependence on Earth's surface.
	12. The process, patterns, and functions of human settlement.
Environment and Society	15. How physical systems affect human systems.
The Uses of Geography	17. How to apply geography to interpret the past.

UNIT 5: LITERACY

The Animal Migrations curriculum aligns with these Common Core ELA aims:

Reading Informational Text: Key Ideas and Details

CCSS.ELA-LITERACY.RI.K.1/1.1
Ask and answer questions about key details in a text.

CCSS.ELA-LITERACY.RI.K.2/1.2
Identify the main topic and retell key details of a text.

CCSS.ELA-LITERACY.RI.K.3/1.3
Describe the connection between two individuals, events, ideas, or pieces of information in a text.

Reading Information: Craft and Structure

CCSS.ELA-LITERACY.RI.K.4/1.4
Ask and answer questions to help determine or clarify the meaning of words and phrases in a text.

CCSS.ELA-LITERACY.RI.K.5
Identify the front cover, back cover, and title page of a book.

CCSS.ELA-LITERACY.RI.1.5
Know and use various text features to locate key facts or information in a text.

CCSS.ELA-LITERACY.RI.1.6
Distinguish between information provided by pictures or other illustrations and information provided by the words in a text.

Reading Information: Integration of Knowledge and Ideas

CCSS.ELA-LITERACY.RI.K.7/1.7
Use the illustrations and details in a text to describe its key ideas.

CCSS.ELA-LITERACY.RI.1.9
Identify basic similarities in and differences between two texts on the same topic.

Reading Information: Range of Reading and Level of Text Complexity	*CCSS.ELA-LITERACY.RI.K.10* Actively engage in group reading activities with purpose and understanding. *CCSS.ELA-LITERACY.RI.1.10* With prompting and support, read grade level informational texts.
Foundational Skills: Print Concepts	*CCSS.ELA-LITERACY.RF.K.1c* Understand that words are separated by spaces in print. *CCSS.ELA-LITERACY.RF.1.1a* Recognize the distinguishing features of a sentence (e.g., first word, capitalization, ending punctuation).
Writing: Text Types and Purposes	*CCSS.ELA-LITERACY.W.K.2/1.2* Write informative/explanatory texts in which they name a topic, supply some facts about the topic, and provide some sense of closure.
Production and Distribution of Writing	*CCSS.ELA-LITERACY.W.K.5/1.5* With guidance and support from adults, focus on a topic, respond to questions and suggestions from peers, and add details to strengthen writing as needed. *CCSS.ELA-LITERACY.W.K.6/1.6* With guidance and support from adults, use a variety of digital tools to produce and publish writing, including in collaboration with peers.
Research to Build and Present Knowledge	*CCSS.ELA-LITERACY.W.K.7/1.7* Participate in shared research and writing projects. *CCSS.ELA-LITERACY.W.K.8/1.8* With guidance and support from adults, recall information from experiences or gather information from provided sources to answer a question.

Speaking and Listening: Comprehension and Collaboration	**CCSS.ELA-LITERACY.SL.K.1/1.1** Participate in collaborative conversations with peers and adults in small and larger groups. **CCSS.ELA-LITERACY.SL.K.2/1.2** Ask and answer questions about key details in a text read aloud or information presented orally or through other media.
Presentation of Knowledge	**CCSS.ELA-LITERACY.SL.K.5/1.5** Add drawings or other visual displays to descriptions when appropriate to clarify ideas.
Language: Conventions of Standard English	**CCSS.ELA-LITERACY.L.K.1f** Produce and expand complete sentences in shared language activities. **CCSS.ELA-LITERACY.L.1.2d** Use conventional spelling for words with common spelling patterns and for frequently occurring irregular words. **CCSS.ELA-LITERACY.L.1.2e** Spell untaught words phonetically, drawing on phonemic awareness and spelling conventions.
Vocabulary Acquisition and Use	**CCSS.ELA-LITERACY.L.K.6/1.6** Use words and phrases acquired through conversations, reading and being read to, and responding to texts.

UNIT 5: MATHEMATICS

The Animal Migrations curriculum aligns with these Common Core Standards for Math Practice:

Math Practice	*CCSS.MATH.PRACTICE.MP1* Make sense of problems and persevere in solving them. *CCSS.MATH.PRACTICE.MP2* Reason abstractly and quantitatively. *CCSS.MATH.PRACTICE.MP4* Model with mathematics. *CCSS.MATH.PRACTICE.MP5* Use appropriate tools strategically.

... and with these Common Core Standards for Math Content:

Operations and Algebraic Thinking	*CCSS.MATH.CONTENT.2.OA.A.1* Use addition and subtraction within 100 to solve word problems.
Numbers and Operations in Base Ten	*CCSS.MATH.CONTENT.2.OBT.A.1* Understand that the three digits of a three-digit number represent amounts of hundreds, tens, and ones.
Measurement and Data	*CCSS.MATH.CONTENT.1.MD.A.2* Express the length of an object as a whole number of length units. *CCSS.MATH.CONTENT.1.MD.C.4* Organize, represent, and interpret data with up to three categories; ask and answer questions about the data points.
Geometry	*CCSS.MATH.CONTENT.K.G.A.3* Identify shapes as two-dimensional or three-dimensional.

UNIT 5: SCIENCE

The Animal Migrations curriculum aligns with these Next Generation Science Standards:

Science and Engineering Practices	Practice 1: Asking questions
	Practice 2: Developing and using models
	Practice 4: Analyzing and Interpreting Data
	Practice 5: Using mathematics and computational thinking
	Practice 7: Engaging in argument from evidence
	Practice 8: Obtaining, evaluating, and communicating Information
Disciplinary Core Ideas in Interdependent Relationships in Ecosystems	LS1C: Organization for Matter and Energy Flow in Organisms
	ESS3.A: Natural Resources
	ESS3.C: Human Impacts on Earth Systems
Disciplinary Core Ideas in Structure and Function	LS1.A: Structure and Function
	LS1.B: Growth and Development of Organisms
	LS1.D: Information Processing
	LS3.A: Inheritance of Traits
	LS3.B: Variation of Traits
Crosscutting Concepts	*Patterns* Patterns in the natural and human designed world can be observed and used as evidence.
	Cause and Effect Events have causes that generate observable patterns.
	Systems and System Models Systems in the natural and designed world have parts that work together.

UNIT 5: GEOGRAPHY

The Animal Migrations curriculum aligns with these National Geography Standards:

The World in Spatial Terms	*1. How to use maps and other geographic representations, tools, and technologies to acquire, process, and report information.*
	2. How to use mental maps to organize information about people, places, and environments.
	3. How to analyze the spatial organization of people, places, and environments on Earth's surface.
Places and Regions	*4. The physical and human characteristics of places.*
Physical Systems	*8. The characteristics and spatial distribution of ecosystems on Earth's surface.*
The Uses of Geography	*18. How to apply geography to interpret the present and plan for the future.*

UNIT 6: LITERACY

The Whales curriculum aligns with these Common Core ELA aims:

Reading Informational Text: Key Ideas and Details

CCSS.ELA-LITERACY.RI.K.1/1.1
Ask and answer questions about key details in a text.

CCSS.ELA-LITERACY.RI.K.2/1.2
Identify the main topic and retell key details of a text.

CCSS.ELA-LITERACY.RI.K.3/1.3
Describe the connection between two individuals, events, ideas, or pieces of information in a text.

Reading Information: Craft and Structure

CCSS.ELA-LITERACY.RI.K.4/1.4
Ask and answer questions to help determine or clarify the meaning of words and phrases in a text.

CCSS.ELA-LITERACY.RI.K.5
Identify the front cover, back cover, and title page of a book.

CCSS.ELA-LITERACY.RI.1.5
Know and use various text features to locate key facts or information in a text.

CCSS.ELA-LITERACY.RI.1.6
Distinguish between information provided by pictures or other illustrations and information provided by the words in a text.

Reading Information: Integration of Knowledge and Ideas

CCSS.ELA-LITERACY.RI.1.7
Use the illustrations and details in a text to describe its key ideas.

CCSS.ELA-LITERACY.RI.1.9
Identify basic similarities in and differences between two texts on the same topic.

Reading Information: Range of Reading and Level of Text Complexity	*CCSS.ELA-LITERACY.RI.K.10* Actively engage in group reading activities with purpose and understanding. *CCSS.ELA-LITERACY.RI.1.10* With prompting and support, read grade level informational texts.
Foundational Skills: Print Concepts	*CCSS.ELA-LITERACY.RF.K.1c* Understand that words are separated by spaces in print. *CCSS.ELA-LITERACY.RF.1.1a* Recognize the distinguishing features of a sentence (e.g., first word, capitalization, ending punctuation).
Writing: Text Types and Purposes	*CCSS.ELA-LITERACY.W.K.2/1.2* Write informative/explanatory texts in which they name a topic, supply some facts about the topic, and provide some sense of closure.
Production and Distribution of Writing	*CCSS.ELA-LITERACY.W.K.5/1.5* With guidance and support from adults, focus on a topic, respond to questions and suggestions from peers, and add details to strengthen writing as needed. *CCSS.ELA-LITERACY.W.K.6/1.6* With guidance and support from adults, use a variety of digital tools to produce and publish writing, including in collaboration with peers.
Research to Build and Present Knowledge	*CCSS.ELA-LITERACY.W.K.7/1.7* Participate in shared research and writing projects. *CCSS.ELA-LITERACY.W.K.8/1.8* With guidance and support from adults, recall information from experiences or gather information from provided sources to answer a question.

Speaking and Listening: Comprehension and Collaboration	CCSS.ELA-LITERACY.SL.K.1/1.1 Participate in collaborative conversations with peers and adults in small and larger groups. CCSS.ELA-LITERACY.SL.K.2/1.2 Ask and answer questions about key details in a text read aloud or information presented orally or through other media. CCSS.ELA-LITERACY.SL.K.3/1.3 Ask and answer questions about what a speaker says in order to gather additional information or clarify something that is not understood.
Presentation of Knowledge	CCSS.ELA-LITERACY.SL.K.4/1.4 Describe people, places, things, and events with relevant details, expressing ideas and feelings clearly. CCSS.ELA-LITERACY.SL.K.5/1.5 Add drawings or other visual displays to descriptions when appropriate to clarify ideas. CCSS.ELA-LITERACY.SL.K.6/1.6 Produce complete sentences when appropriate to task and situation.
Language: Conventions of Standard English	CCSS.ELA-LITERACY.L.K.1f Produce and expand complete sentences in shared language activities. CCSS.ELA-LITERACY.L.1.2b Use end punctuation for sentences. CCSS.ELA-LITERACY.L.1.2d Use conventional spelling for words with common spelling patterns and for frequently occurring irregular words. CCSS.ELA-LITERACY.L.1.2e Spell untaught words phonetically, drawing on phonemic awareness and spelling conventions.
Vocabulary Acquisition and Use	CCSS.ELA-LITERACY.L.K.6/1.6 Use words and phrases acquired through conversations, reading and being read to, and responding to texts.

UNIT 6: MATHEMATICS

The Whales curriculum aligns with these Common Core Standards for Math Practice:

Math Practice	*CCSS.MATH.PRACTICE.MP1* Make sense of problems and persevere in solving them. *CCSS.MATH.PRACTICE.MP2* Reason abstractly and quantitatively. *CCSS.MATH.PRACTICE.MP4* Model with mathematics. *CCSS.MATH.PRACTICE.MP5* Use appropriate tools strategically. *CCSS.MATH.PRACTICE.MP6* Attend to precision. *CCSS.MATH.PRACTICE.MP7* Look for and make use of structure.

... and with these Common Core Standards for Math Content:

Operations and Algebraic Thinking	*CCSS.MATH.CONTENT.1.OA.A.1* Use addition and subtraction to solve word problems by using objects, drawings, and equations with a symbol for the unknown number to represent the problem.
Numbers and Operations in Base Ten	*CCSS.MATH.CONTENT.1.NBT.B.3* Compare two numbers based on meanings of the digits.
Measurement and Data	*CCSS.MATH.CONTENT.2.MD.A.1* Measure the length of an object by selecting and using appropriate tools such as rulers, yardsticks, meter sticks, and measuring tapes. *CCSS.MATH.CONTENT.1.MD.A.1* Order three objects by length; compare the lengths of two objects indirectly by using a third object.

Measurement and Data, cont'd	CCSS.MATH.CONTENT.1.MD.A.2 Express the length of an object as a whole number of length units. CCSS.MATH.CONTENT.1.MD.B.3 Tell and write time. CCSS.MATH.CONTENT.1.MD.C.4 Organize, represent, and interpret data with up to three categories; ask and answer questions about the total number of data points, how many in each category, and how many more or less are in one category than in another.
Geometry	CCSS.MATH.CONTENT.K.G.A.3 Identify shapes as two-dimensional or three-dimensional.

UNIT 6: SCIENCE

The Whales curriculum aligns with these Next Generation Science Standards:

Science and Engineering Practices	Practice 1: Asking questions Practice 2: Developing and using models Practice 3: Planning and carrying out investigations Practice 4: Analyzing and Interpreting Data Practice 5: Using mathematics and computational thinking Practice 6: Constructing explanations Practice 7: Engaging in argument from evidence Practice 8: Obtaining, evaluating, and communicating Information

Disciplinary Core Ideas in Interdependent Relationships in Ecosystems	LS1C: Organization for Matter and Energy Flow in Organisms ESS3.A: Natural Resources ESS3.C: Human Impacts on Earth Systems
Disciplinary Core Ideas in Waves	PS4.A: Wave Properties
Disciplinary Core Ideas in Structure and Function	LS1.A: Structure and Function LS1.B: Growth and Development of Organisms LS1.D: Information Processing LS3.A: Inheritance of Traits LS3.B: Variation of Traits
Disciplinary Core Ideas in Engineering Design	ETS1.A: Defining and Delimiting Engineering Problems ETS1.B: Developing Possible Solutions ETS1.C: Optimizing the Design Solution
Crosscutting Concepts	*Patterns* Patterns in the natural and human designed world can be observed and used as evidence. *Cause and Effect* Events have causes that generate observable patterns. *Systems and System Models* Systems in the natural and designed world have parts that work together. *Structure and Function* The shape and stability of structures of natural and designed objects are related to their function(s).

UNIT 6: GEOGRAPHY

The Whales curriculum aligns with these National Geography Standards:

The World in Spatial Terms	1. How to use maps and other geographic representations, tools, and technologies to acquire, process, and report information.
	2. How to use mental maps to organize information about people, places, and environments.
	3. How to analyze the spatial organization of people, places, and environments on Earth's surface.
Places and Regions	4. The physical and human characteristics of places.
Physical Systems	8. The characteristics and spatial distribution of ecosystems on Earth's surface.
Environment and Society	14. How human actions modify the physical environment.
The Uses of Geography	18. How to apply geography to interpret the present and plan for the future.

UNIT 7: LITERACY

The Greeks curriculum aligns with these Common Core ELA aims:

Reading Literature:
Key Ideas and Details

CCSS.ELA-LITERACY.RI.K.1/1.1
Ask and answer questions about key details in a text.

CCSS.ELA-LITERACY.RI.K.2/1.2
Retell stories, including key details, and demonstrate understanding of their central message or lesson.

CCSS.ELA-LITERACY.RI.K.3/1.3
Describe characters, settings, and major events in a story, using key details.

Reading Literature:
Craft and Structure

CCSS.ELA-LITERACY.RI.K.4/1.4
Identify words and phrases in stories or poems that suggest feelings or appeal to the senses.

CCSS.ELA-LITERACY.RL.K.5/1.5
Explain major differences between books that tell stories and books that give information, drawing on a wide reading of a range of text types.

CCSS.ELA-LITERACY.RL.1.6
Identify who is telling the story at various points in a text.

Reading Literature:
Integration of Knowledge and Ideas

CCSS.ELA-LITERACY.RI.1.7
Use the illustrations and details in a text to describe its characters, setting, or events.

CCSS.ELA-LITERACY.RL.K.9/1.9
Compare and contrast the adventures and experiences of characters in stories.

Reading Literature:
Range of Reading and
Level of Text Complexity

CCSS.ELA-LITERACY.RI.K.10
Actively engage in group reading activities with purpose and understanding.

JOURNEYS

Reading Informational Text: Key Ideas and Details	**CCSS.ELA-LITERACY.RI.K.1/1.1** Ask and answer questions about key details in a text. **CCSS.ELA-LITERACY.RI.K.2/1.2** Identify the main topic and retell key details of a text. **CCSS.ELA-LITERACY.RI.K.3/1.3** Describe the connection between two individuals, events, ideas, or pieces of information in a text.
Reading Information: Craft and Structure	**CCSS.ELA-LITERACY.RI.K.4/1.4** Ask and answer questions to help determine or clarify the meaning of words and phrases in a text. **CCSS.ELA-LITERACY.RI.1.5** Know and use various text features to locate key facts or information in a text. **CCSS.ELA-LITERACY.RI.1.6** Distinguish between information provided by pictures or other illustrations and information provided by the words in a text.
Reading Information: Integration of Knowledge and Ideas	**CCSS.ELA-LITERACY.RI.1.7** Use the illustrations and details in a text to describe its key ideas. **CCSS.ELA-LITERACY.RI.1.9** Identify basic similarities in and differences between two texts on the same topic.
Reading Information: Range of Reading and Level of Text Complexity	**CCSS.ELA-LITERACY.RI.K.10** Actively engage in group reading activities with purpose and understanding. **CCSS.ELA-LITERACY.RI.1.10** With prompting and support, read grade level informational texts.

Foundational Skills: Print Concepts	*CCSS.ELA-LITERACY.RF.K.1c* Understand that words are separated by spaces in print. *CCSS.ELA-LITERACY.RF.1.1a* Recognize the distinguishing features of a sentence (e.g., first word, capitalization, ending punctuation).
Writing: Text Types and Purposes	*CCSS.ELA-LITERACY.W.K.3/1.3* Write narratives in which they recount two or more appropriately sequenced events, include some details regarding what happened, use temporal words to signal event order, and provide some sense of closure.
Production and Distribution of Writing	*CCSS.ELA-LITERACY.W.K.5/1.5* With guidance and support from adults, focus on a topic, respond to questions and suggestions from peers, and add details to strengthen writing as needed. *CCSS.ELA-LITERACY.W.K.6/1.6* With guidance and support from adults, use a variety of digital tools to produce and publish writing, including in collaboration with peers.
Research to Build and Present Knowledge	*CCSS.ELA-LITERACY.W.K.7/1.7* Participate in shared research and writing projects. *CCSS.ELA-LITERACY.W.K.8/1.8* With guidance and support from adults, recall information from experiences or gather information from provided sources to answer a question.

Speaking and Listening: Comprehension and Collaboration	CCSS.ELA-LITERACY.SL.K.1/1.1 Participate in collaborative conversations with peers and adults in small and larger groups. CCSS.ELA-LITERACY.SL.K.2/1.2 Ask and answer questions about key details in a text read aloud or information presented orally or through other media. CCSS.ELA-LITERACY.SL.K.3/1.3 Ask and answer questions about what a speaker says in order to gather additional information or clarify something that is not understood.
Presentation of Knowledge	CCSS.ELA-LITERACY.SL.K.4/1.4 Describe people, places, things, and events with relevant details, expressing ideas and feelings clearly. CCSS.ELA-LITERACY.SL.K.5/1.5 Add drawings or other visual displays to descriptions when appropriate to clarify ideas. CCSS.ELA-LITERACY.SL.K.6/1.6 Produce complete sentences when appropriate to task and situation.
Language: Conventions of Standard English	CCSS.ELA-LITERACY.L.K.1f Produce and expand complete sentences in shared language activities. CCSS.ELA-LITERACY.L.1.2d Use conventional spelling for words with common spelling patterns and for frequently occurring irregular words. CCSS.ELA-LITERACY.L.1.2e Spell untaught words phonetically, drawing on phonemic awareness and spelling conventions.
Vocabulary Acquisition and Use	CCSS.ELA-LITERACY.L.K.6/1.6 Use words and phrases acquired through conversations, reading and being read to, and responding to texts.

UNIT 7: MATHEMATICS

The Greeks curriculum aligns with these Common Core Standards for Math Practice:

Math Practice	*CCSS.MATH.PRACTICE.MP1* Make sense of problems and persevere in solving them. *CCSS.MATH.PRACTICE.MP2* Reason abstractly and quantitatively. *CCSS.MATH.PRACTICE.MP3* Construct viable arguments and critique the reasoning of others. *CCSS.MATH.PRACTICE.MP4* Model with mathematics. *CCSS.MATH.PRACTICE.MP5* Use appropriate tools strategically. *CCSS.MATH.PRACTICE.MP6* Attend to precision. *CCSS.MATH.PRACTICE.MP7* Look for and make use of structure. *CCSS.MATH.PRACTICE.MP8* Look for and express regularity in repeated reasoning.

... and with these Common Core Standards for Math Content:

Operations and Algebraic Thinking	*CCSS.MATH.CONTENT.1.OA.A.1* Use addition and subtraction to solve word problems by using objects, drawings, and equations with a symbol for the unknown number to represent the problem. *CCSS.MATH.CONTENT.2.OA.B.4* Use addition to find the total number of objects arranged in rectangular arrays; write an equation to express the total as a sum of equal addends. *CCSS.MATH.CONTENT.3.OA.A.1* Interpret products of whole numbers. *CCSS.MATH.CONTENT.3.OA.D.9* Identify arithmetic patterns and explain them using properties of operations.

Numbers and Operations in Base Ten

CCSS.MATH.CONTENT.1.NBT.B.2
Understand that the two digits of a two-digit number represent amounts of tens and ones.

CCSS.MATH.CONTENT.1.NBT.B.3
Compare two two-digit numbers based on meanings of the tens and ones digits.

CCSS.MATH.CONTENT.2.NBT.B.5
Fluently add and subtract within 100 using strategies based on place value, properties of operations, and/or the relationship between addition and subtraction.

Measurement and Data

CCSS.MATH.CONTENT.3.MD.C.5
Recognize area as an attribute of plane figures and understand concepts of area measurement.

CCSS.MATH.CONTENT.3.MD.C.6
Measure areas by counting unit squares.

CCSS.MATH.CONTENT.3.MD.C.7
Relate area to the operations of multiplication and addition.

CCSS.MATH.CONTENT.3.MD.D.8
Solve real world and mathematical problems involving perimeters of polygons.

Geometry

CCSS.MATH.CONTENT.K.G.A.1
Describe objects in the environment using names of shapes.

CCSS.MATH.CONTENT.K.G.A.2
Correctly name shapes regardless of their orientations or overall size.

CCSS.MATH.CONTENT.K.G.A.3
Identify shapes as two-dimensional or three-dimensional.

CCSS.MATH.CONTENT.K.G.B.4
Analyze and compare two- and three-dimensional shapes, in different sizes and orientations, using informal language to describe their similarities, differences, parts and other attributes.

Geometry, cont'd	*CCSS.MATH.CONTENT.K.G.B.5* Model shapes in the world by building shapes from components and drawing shapes. *CCSS.MATH.CONTENT.K.G.B.6* Compose simple shapes to form larger shapes. *CCSS.MATH.CONTENT.2.G.A.2* Partition a rectangle into rows and columns of same-size squares and count to find the total number of them.

UNIT 6: SCIENCE

The Greeks curriculum aligns with these Next Generation Science Standards:

Science and Engineering Practices	*Practice 1: Asking questions* *Practice 2: Developing and using models* *Practice 4: Analyzing and Interpreting Data* *Practice 5: Using mathematics and computational thinking* *Practice 6: Constructing explanations* *Practice 7: Engaging in argument from evidence*
Disciplinary Core Ideas in Engineering Design	*ETS1.A: Defining and Delimiting Engineering Problems* *ETS1.B: Developing Possible Solutions*
Crosscutting Concepts	*Structure and Function* The shape and stability of structures of natural and designed objects are related to their function(s).

UNIT 7: GEOGRAPHY

The Greeks curriculum aligns with these National Geography Standards:

The World in Spatial Terms

1. How to use maps and other geographic representations, tools, and technologies to acquire, process, and report information.

2. How to use mental maps to organize information about people, places, and environments.

3. How to analyze the spatial organization of people, places, and environments on Earth's surface.

Places and Regions

4. The physical and human characteristics of places.

6. How culture and experience influence people's perception of places and regions.

Human Systems

10. The characteristics, distributions, and complexity of Earth's cultural mosaics.

12. The process, patterns, and functions of human settlement.

13. How forces of cooperation and conflict among people influence the division and control of Earth's surface.

Environment and Society

15. How physical systems affect human systems.

The Uses of Geography

17. How to apply geography to interpret the past.